WHAT PEOPLE ARE

The Faith

CW01066607

I've read lots of books on faith and doing the "
theology, how to's and how not to's. But what Steve Long writes is clearly
to do as well. It's so simple, and Steve breaks it down so clearly that anyone can move into the
Faith Zone. He leaves us without excuse! And it is written from his own experience including
many stories of miraculous breakthroughs in multiple areas. I love it. I want the first copy!

BARBARA YODER
Lead Apostle, Shekinah Regional Apostolic Center

Pastor Steve Long has written an extraordinary book on faith to give today's Christians an
understanding of how great men and women in the Bible exercise faith to obtain their blessings. This book gives us a picture of the historical Jesus of Nazareth interacting with His original audience and how they received miracles, deliverances and healing because of their faith.

This book will move the reader to step out in faith as they grab a hold of their personal
revelation of the word of God. Pastor Long has done an excellent and balanced exposition
on faith based on the Gospels. This book will ignite and activate the reader's' faith to do the
impossible.

I endorse this book to be read by all pastors, ministry leaders and everyone. We need faith
based on the revelation of the Word of God to fulfill the plans and purposes of God for our
lives, ministry and destiny.

BISHOP BOB TACKY
Presiding Bishop, Impact Lives Church Canada

Faith is one of the most powerful elements of the Kingdom. In this book Steve Long gives
simple but profound truths about faith that, if applied, will bring you to your next level.
It is scripturally based, revelatory and easy to understand. Thank you so much Steve for this
wonderful equipping tool for the Body of Christ!

FAYTENE GRASSESCHI
Director of The CRY, and MY Canada Association

The Faith Zone is an energetic treasure! It catapults faith from the realm of theory to a living
impartation. Steve Long has created a masterpiece in linking divine revelation to the arena
of faith. He has given us a book that spans the range between the simplistic to the profound.
One learns that anyone can grow and reap the rewards of walking in greater dimensions
of faith.

I highly recommend this powerful read. It will place you into a whole new realm of Holy Spirit activity. Signs and wonders will follow. It will equip you to become a world changer!

DR. GEORGE D. JOHNSON
George Johnson Ministries International
Convening Apostle, Canadian Coalition of Apostolic Leaders

We have known Steve for many years now and have benefitted from his unique way of bringing seemingly complicated concepts of the kingdom into realms of understanding that children can grasp. The reason this book will change your life is because of the example that Steve sets in his actions and lifestyle, which will challenge and change you. To have this wisdom written in a book just means you can follow his example more clearly. It is gold for the body of Christ!

Steve has written this book is such a simple and straightforward manner which is how he sees the kingdom. His faith is straightforward and he allows you to walk in that simplicity.

You will be challenged by this read, not just by the enormity of the possibilities but also by the ease of the journey!

STUART & CHLOE GLASSBOROW
Lead Pastors, Catch The Fire London
Directors, The Kenyan Children's Project

Faith is the prerequisite to experiencing a life of miracles, provision and the power of God. Steve Long is a man of faith who has experienced the breakthrough of God's power for himself by cultivating a faith-filled life. As Steve walks us through Gospel accounts of faith in his excellent and practical new book, he helps us see that a life of faith is within the grasp of every believer as we learn to act on the revelation of who God is and what He has promised. A must-read for all who want to embark on a journey to the realm of great faith!

WES HALL
Acting President, International House of Prayer University

Steve has a great Biblical teaching gift with a style full of revelation. He has an ability to set the scene for you in Jesus' time and captivate you with the stories of faith found therein. Steve's practical guidance and faith steps, along with many personal testimonies will lead you to want a greater experience of faith for your own life. This is a thorough Bible study you don't want to miss for your own personal growth and your study group.

DUNCAN & KATE SMITH
Presidents, Catch The Fire World
Senior Leaders, Catch The Fire Raleigh

The Faith Zone

The Faith Zone
Published by Catch The Fire Books
272 Attwell Drive, Toronto ON M9W 6M3 Canada

Distributed worldwide by Catch The Fire Distribution. Titles may be purchased in bulk; for information, please contact distribution@catchthefire.com.

Catch The Fire® is a registered trademark of Catch The Fire World.

All rights reserved. Except for brief excerpts for review purposes, no part of this book may be reproduced or used in any form or media without written permission from the publisher.

Any website addresses recommended throughout this book are offered as a resource to you. These websites are not intended in any way to imply an endorsement on the part of Catch The Fire, nor do we vouch for their content. The information in this book was correct at the time it was published.

All scripture quotations, unless otherwise indicated, are taken from the Holy Bible, New International Version®, NIV®. Copyright ©1973, 1978, 1984, 2011 by Biblica, Inc.™ Used by permission of Zondervan. All rights reserved worldwide. www.zondervan.com The "NIV" and "New International Version" are trademarks registered in the United States Patent and Trademark Office by Biblica, Inc.™

Scripture quotations marked NASB are taken from the New American Standard Bible®, Copyright © 1960, 1962, 1963, 1968, 1971, 1972, 1973, 1975, 1977, 1995 by The Lockman Foundation Used by permission. (www.Lockman.org)

Scripture quotations from THE MESSAGE. Copyright © by Eugene H. Peterson 1993, 1994, 1995, 1996, 2000, 2001, 2002. Used by permission of NavPress Publishing Group.

Scripture quotations marked KJV are taken from the King James Version (Public Domain).

ISBN 978-1-894310-87-1
Copyright © 2016 Steve Long

The Team: Luke Richards, Nicole Briand, Christy Markham, Volodymyra Garmazonova, Marcott Bernarde, Benjamin Jackson, Jonathan Puddle
Editor: Noel Gruber
Cover design: Volodymyra Garmazonova and Marcott Bernarde (Catch The Fire)
Interior layout: Medlar Publishing Solutions Pvt Ltd, India

Printed in Canada
First Edition 2016

THE

Faith

ZONE

STEVE LONG

WITH MARK VIRKLER

CATCH THE FIRE
BOOKS

Contents

Foreword

The Faith Zone is a wonderful book, making the complex simple and the unreachable practical. For many, faith is a very intimidating subject. Tragically, it is often thought to be out of reach to the average believer. Because of this, *The Faith Zone* will become an extremely important tool in assisting the Church to step more fully into what we were created for—faith in God. In a sense, faith is the outcome of a relationship with God. In this relationship, we are to interact with him, know him, enjoy and delight in him. But all of these aspects of our lives are based on trust. In knowing him, we find that he is absolutely trustworthy. Faith, then, is simply an expression of trust towards the One who is trustworthy.

Faith is one of the most important subjects in all of life. This one realm gives us access to favor from God that few other things can provide. And while he loves everyone the same, not everyone has the same favor. Increasing in favor with God is what we all need, continually. Hebrews 11:6 puts it this way, "And without faith it is impossible to please Him, for he who comes to God must believe that He is and that He is a rewarder of those who seek Him." To say that faith must be present and active for us to be pleasing to God is a strong statement. That proclamation is followed by an important clarification—it's not enough only to believe he exists. The devil believes that much. We must believe He is a rewarder. Putting it another way, we must believe in his nature as a good Father, which in part is his virtue of rewarding those who seek and trust him.

To the renewed mind, faith is logical because it is based on who he is. A key thought presented on these pages is that faith is simply acting on the revelation of God. I love that! Faith will only explore what revelation reveals. When we said yes to the invitation to follow Jesus, we embarked on a journey. It's a journey to find out what might be possible in our lifetime if we truly believe in who he is and what he has promised. Leonard Ravenhill is quoted as saying, *"One of these days some simple soul will pick up the Book of God, read it, and believe it. Then the rest of us will be embarrassed."* That statement is not quoted to bring shame, but to stir up passion to discover what God has made available to all who follow—to all who believe.

The author, Steve Long, wrote this book with the desire to spark hope in the reader that he or she might move into what he calls *the faith zone*. That's the realm where nothing is impossible. Steve is one of the best equipping and empowering pastors that I know of, anywhere. His delight is for others to experience what many have thought to be for leaders only. In reading *The Faith Zone,* you will see that he has successfully taken the challenge of making this subject doable. If you're anything like me, you want to grow in faith, and in the process become known by God as a person of great faith. He deserves it, as he is perfectly faithful, trustworthy, honest, and filled with hope for our own future.

I love the format of this book. In one sense it is a Bible study, mostly from the Gospel of Matthew. But it's not a study to fill our minds with mere facts or unimportant details. It is a study to introduce us to the Faithful One, and in turn increase our confidence in who he is and what he has said. I believe this book will stir up the faith and hope of all who read it. The miracle stories of Scripture come alive as the author breaks them down into practical bite-size pieces. The author then writes of some of his own miracle stories to bring the application of Scripture closer to home.

Steve Long has done all of us a huge favor by putting his insights, or more correctly, his life, into print. I can't imagine anyone reading this book and not coming away with greater confidence in God and a greater passion to please him by living in the *faith zone*.

Bill Johnson
Bethel Church, Redding, California
Author of *When Heaven Invades Earth* and *The Power that Changes the World*

Acknowledgements

Sandra and I have one of the best jobs on this planet! We get to lead Catch The Fire Toronto. Our people are amazing; they are full of faith. They inspire us all the time.

While I have the title of Senior Leader, it is the church-goers and my fellow pastors who are the ones teaching me. I hear stories most weeks that are over the top. Stories of people who are doing great exploits because they had a revelation from Father God and dared to believe it could be true.

Here are a couple of examples.

A lady was diagnosed with more than 50 tumours in her abdomen and put in palliative care immediately. One night she had a dream where the Lord told her she was healed. The next morning, she asked to go home. Long story short: after going through all the tests again, all the tumours had disappeared. She continues to be tumour free!

A man was at church on a Sunday morning. A second offering was taken to bless one of the pastors. He felt the Lord saying to give an amount that for him was large. He did. Long story short: when he got home from the meeting, there was an envelope in his mailbox with money matching his gift!

A lady was driving home and saw homeless people in a downtown Toronto park. She felt the Lord saying that she should feed them and talk about the love of Jesus. The next week she took food with her on the same trip home. That was twenty years ago. Long story short: she now leads a charity that serves hundreds of people each week. She has full-time staff with her, many volunteers, and God pays all the bills!

A man was in the middle of bankruptcy. His business was not doing well. He heard a talk at our church on tithing. He wasn't a giver but decided to trust God. He went to the bank and withdrew the exact tithe, down to the last penny of his last pay cheque. He gave it the next Sunday. After the meeting, as he was walking to his car, a man gave him an envelope of cash. It was the exact amount, to the penny, of what he had just given to the Lord. Long story short: he continues to be generous and is now one of the top income earners in Canada!

A man was having his time with God on a Monday morning. As he was soaking and journaling the Lord began to give him a download that lasted almost three hours. It was mostly numbers and math computations. Long story short: it took him three months to figure out that the Lord has just given him the computer code to a new software program. He sells the software for $100,000 per unit!

Thank you Catch The Fire Toronto for inspiring me!

Mark Virkler helped to transform my life! My first seminar at Catch The Fire in 1993 was a prophetic school and Mark was one of the speakers. He taught hearing God's voice via journaling. At that time I didn't journal and more importantly, I didn't believe that God was still speaking.

Mark changed all of that within the first ten minutes of his seminar. I have been on speaking terms with Father God since that time. So, when I was pondering the "next steps" process at the end of each chapter I felt to ask Mark if he would write the journaling exercises. Mark said yes. His insights and questions take my theory into the practical. Thank you Mark!

Thanks again to the Catch The Fire team for their work in this project. Thanks to Noel Gruber for editing this, my third book with her help. Perhaps I will get her to write the next one and she simply puts my name on it!

Thank you Sandra for letting me take time to write books. Love you!

Thank you Father God for speaking and giving us revelation. Thank you for inspiring us to move hope into the faith zone!

Welcome to The Faith Zone!

People have lots of reasons for writing a book. Some write to make money; though that rarely happens. Some write to become famous. (If famous means boxes of unsold books in a basement, then yes!)

I wrote this book because the Lord asked me to. I felt God say that the revelations he had given me would help others understand how faith works. So, in May of 2014, I did what the Lord told me to do: I booked a cruise for my wife Sandra and I, and on the ship I began to write. Because the cruise was thirteen days, this book has thirteen chapters.

I'm a morning person, while Sandra loves to sleep in, take her time, visit the spa, etc. So every morning I found a corner table in one of the coffee shops and began to look at this topic of faith. Sandra would come find me around noon, and we'd hit the buffet together.

The revelation that I received about faith can be summarized like this: Faith is acting on revelation. When we receive a God-thought, hope almost always rises up in our spirit. While hope is good, it isn't enough on its own. In fact, if hope is all we get to and we do nothing beyond it, we will soon be depressed and discouraged. Proverbs 13:12 tells us, *"Hope deferred makes the heart sick, but a longing fulfilled is a tree of life."*

Hope is the appetizer before a great meal. Hope is the adrenalin that

motivates us to go a step further than simply dreaming. Hope is the inspiration to act!

Along the way obstacles pop up. Things happen that get in our way. Circumstances and people will oppose the hope that we have. But, if we push
through, we begin to live by faith. Living by faith leads us into an amazing zone where miracles happen! Relational challenges simply disappear.
Financial obstacles are overcome. Health issues vanish.

This is how Jesus lived. He heard from his Father, did what He said, and
saw miracles on a daily basis. This is how we are supposed to live.

I'm going to take you on a journey through the Gospel of Matthew. Most
of the chapters in this book are based on people whom Jesus met. When
Jesus saw how they responded to God's revelations, he made comments.
Jesus told two people that they had "great faith." To others he said "little
faith." To some he said "no faith." We'll look at their stories and why Jesus
said what he did.

I recently had a new revelation. You may have already seen this one, but
for me it was inspiring. In Matthew 9:5 Jesus asked this question: "*Which
is easier: to say, 'Your sins are forgiven,' or to say, 'Get up and walk'?*"

How could it be easier to heal a man crippled for most of his life than to
simply say he was forgiven?

Here is what the Father said to me. It was easy, because the four friends
who brought the lame man to Jesus had done the hard work. When Jesus

saw their faith, their acting on revelation, He too stepped into action and ministered to the man.

Jesus knew that the breakthrough into the faith zone had already happened. He saw it on their faces. These four men had persevered through obstacles to get their friend to Jesus. Because they did the hard work, the final step of declaring the man healed was the easy part!

I trust that as you read my attempt to explain faith, you will be enlightened, inspired, and provoked. My prayer is that faith would move from difficult to easy and that miracles and breakthroughs would happen in your life and in your ministry as a result.

Blessings,
Steve Long
May 2016

CHAPTER 1

What Faith is all About

HEBREWS 11

Walt Disney was a dreamer. He was perhaps the first person to conceive that animals and plants could speak in cartoons. He dreamed of bringing fun and big smiles to children of all ages. He dreamed of theme parks where everyone could be a child.

A 1949 *Guideposts* magazine quoted Disney on his Christian faith: "Without inspiration, we would perish. All I ask of myself, 'Live a good Christian life.' To that objective I bend every effort in shaping my personal, domestic, and professional activities and growth."[1]

One of Disney's most famous quotes is "all our dreams can come true, if we have the courage to pursue them."[2] The story goes that when the Epcot Centre in Florida opened, a reporter asked if Disney would have been disappointed to not be alive to see it. The spokesperson for Epcot simply replied, "He saw it first."

Disney understood the concept of faith. He grasped that when God gives us dreams, they are within reach because they are actually His dreams.

I grew up thinking that only the super spiritual could understand faith. I felt that living by faith was extremely hard. It isn't. Faith is simply having confidence in something you already know about. It is acting on a revelation.

Now faith is confidence in what we hope for and assurance about what we do not see. This is what the ancients were commended for. **HEBREWS 11:1-2**

Hebrews 11 is one of the classic chapters in the whole Bible. If we were to simplify the Bible to ten chapters, this would be one that I would pick to be in that elite list.

In this magnificent chapter we have multiple examples of how the ancients, the people who lived before us, acted on revelation. Because they knew things, they were able to do things. Great things. Amazing things. They entered the Faith Zone.

We are called by God to live by faith (2 Corinthians 5:7). It is an expectation that our Father has for each one of us. He wants us to know how faith works so we can live in it. He wants us in the Faith Zone so we can bless others and be rewarded by Him.

Somehow, faith has become a challenging word. But faith is not supposed to be difficult. Little children can enter in. New followers of Jesus can get into the Faith Zone.

WHAT IS FAITH?

Before we look at the example of the ancients, let's define what faith is. Hebrews 11:1 says it simply: *"Faith is confidence."* We define the word *confidence* as something that we are absolutely sure of. It is a done deal. It is going to happen, and we know it.

"Confidence in what we hope for"

This confidence that we walk and live is based on a hope. So what is hope? Hope is an idea, a concept, that has come into our spirit. We haven't yet seen it come to fruition, but we are excited for the possibilities. We are optimistic that if it happens, it will be amazing.

Hope is what comes when we have a dream, when we have a bright idea, or when we hear something that sparks life in us. Hope is always about the future. The future may be as close as today or as far as decades away. Hope breathes confidence.

If I can summarize it, hope is a revelation. Probably the simplest way for me to describe it is this: Pretend that you have a dream. In the dream Jesus appears to you with details about the next lottery. He tells you what the winning numbers are. You see Jesus write them on a piece of paper.

I don't play lotteries, nor do I encourage others to, but if I did I would be very excited to know the winning numbers. We all would be very hopeful as we woke up and began to dream of what we could do with the money.

We would begin to imagine. We would be absolutely excited with the possibilities of winning the big one.

We would spend the day thinking of how to use the money. Who am I going to bless? What charities would I support? Can I set up a foundation for my kids and grandchildren so they are looked after for the rest of their lives?

Are you tracking with me? I bet you can picture how excited you would be. That is hope. Hope is strongly linked to faith. According to the writer of Hebrews, *"Faith is confidence in what we hope for"* (v 1).

So if I get a God-thought, that very revelation should spark hope in me. Most of us don't have a problem with the hope part, what we struggle with is the confidence part.

We've had life disappoint us way too many times to have what we call childlike faith. This is hope's negative side. Hope can diminish. It can fade over time if what we are hoping for doesn't happen. Proverbs 13:12 says, *"hope deferred makes the heart sick."*

We can give up believing that our hopes will come to pass. Am I right?

I have good news: This book was written just for you. My goal is to spark hope in your spirit again so that you can go to the next step and move into the Faith Zone.

If indeed it is Father God who put the idea in my head, who gave me the dream, who put the thought in my spirit, well then, maybe I can be confident? The writer of Hebrews disagrees. No maybes. Be convinced!

"Assurance about what we do not see"

Assurance and confidence are very similar. Assurance is based on the person who gave us their word. We have confidence in what they said. These two words are tied together.

Faith is linked to confidence. Faith is linked to hope. Hope is linked to stuff that isn't seen naturally; rather it is revelatory. Our concepts, ideas, and thoughts are all revelations from God.

Our hopes are usually personal. Very few people get the same dreams as you do. We don't all get to work one morning and find that everyone has had a dream where Jesus reveals the winning lottery numbers.

As a result, not everyone will see what you see when you share an idea with them. Their minds won't understand your excitement and hope. Why not? Because they didn't get the revelation. More often than not, people don't get our hopes. Friends, spouses, and colleagues want to see, touch, and know. They need hard facts, research, case studies, etc.

The people who join with you in your hope are the ones who see what you see. We have a name for people like these; we call them dreamers. Another name for them is entrepreneurs. Entrepreneurs are not afraid to step out, to take a chance on something that isn't proven. They will take great risks because they have confidence in an idea.

On a thirteen day cruise, my wife, Sandra, and I were seated beside a German couple for dinner each evening. We had great conversations over the two weeks on the ship. It turned out they are followers of Jesus. He is an entrepreneur, and wow, does he see and hear well!

The gentleman told us about his life, how he started out as a chef, became a restaurant consultant, and then began managing hotels. He told us that he would "see" things that needed to be changed and improved. As he acted on these impressions and thoughts, he made money—lots of it.

In retrospect, as a new believer in Jesus, he understood that God was the one who had given him the creative ideas. The ideas that he got and is still getting have made him a multimillionaire. For example, he's such a big deal that you will find his name listed on the patent for PayPal.

He told us that on a recent flight to Germany he sat beside one of the founders of Google. He shared an idea to improve Google with the executive. The executive wrote him a cheque for $2 million dollars, right there on the plane!

If you are the type of person who has to know everything, you probably won't be a person who walks by faith. Faith is strongly tied to sensing and feeling. Often these ideas and concepts that come to us are nebulous, not always concrete.

Let me summarize Hebrews 11:1 for you as I see it: Faith is simply acting on a revelation. Faith starts with a hope, a revelation. It can stay that way or it can mature to faith. If we begin to act on the revelation, that is when we step from hope to faith.

In my book *On the Run*, I talk about the process David had to go through to become a person after God's heart. He passed through three years of character development and refinement while on the run from King Saul. In one of the chapters I tell the story of how Sandra and I got our first house.

I'll summarize what I wrote. Sandra had several dreams about us being given a home. The dreams brought hope to her. We had been lifelong renters and the idea of owning a home was simply that, an idea. When she shared the dreams with her loving husband (that's me), I didn't respond well. I said things like, "I don't think so." My problem, among others, was a lack of revelation on this house thing. I didn't doubt that Sandra had had a dream from God, but there was no spark that hit me. There should have been, but doubt had sucked a lot of my hope away. I wasn't operating in a lifestyle of faith.

It wasn't until I had a dream about our future house that I actively engaged and began to have confidence in our hope. While Sandra's dream sparked hope, my dream contained the action step: Sandra and I were supposed to give away $1000. The condition God spoke to me for us getting a home was to give the money to someone who was about to purchase their first home. We did that despite being in massive debt. We decided to act with confidence on our revelation.

Long story short, we miraculously received more than $100,000 shortly afterwards, which allowed us to purchase our first home. By doing what we heard, we moved into the Faith Zone, where the impossible happens.

God gave us hope via two dreams. We had confidence in them. We acted on them, though it was difficult. Boom shakalaka, we were rewarded for our faith.

We can step into the Faith Zone. This is the place where God can and does change the rules. It is a wonderful place to live! I love this stuff. It is actually a lot of fun to live this way.

"This is what the ancients were commended for"

The Bible profiles people who lived centuries ago. The writer of Hebrews calls them the ancients (v 2). Many of their faith stories are summarized in Hebrews 11. Each segment in this amazing chapter tells us how men and women, both young and old, received revelations from God and how, with confidence, they acted on their hope.

As you read the stories, I invite you to begin to hope. Begin to make their stories your story. Begin to expect that you too can live this way. One of the primary reasons there are so many personal stories in the Scriptures is to raise our hopes and expectations. God wants us to believe for breakthroughs. What kind of breakthrough do you need?

I am going to take some liberties with the Biblical text. What I am going to do is substitute my definition of faith (acting on a revelation) for the word *faith*. I trust that reading my definition instead of the word *faith* will bring new meaning to you. Let's look at a few examples.

ABEL

By **acting on a revelation** Abel brought God a better offering than Cain did. By **acting on a revelation** he was commended as righteous, when God spoke well of his offerings. And by **acting on a revelation** Abel still speaks, even though he is dead. HEBREWS 11:4

ENOCH

By **acting on a revelation** Enoch was taken from this life, so that he did not experience death: "He could not be found, because God had taken him away." For before he was taken, he was commended as one who pleased God. HEBREWS 11:5

NOAH

By **acting on a revelation** Noah, when warned about things not yet seen, in holy fear built an ark to save his family. By his **acting on a revelation** he condemned the world and became heir of the righteousness that is in keeping with **acting on a revelation**. HEBREWS 11:7

ABRAHAM AND SARAH

By **acting on a revelation** Abraham, when called to go to a place he would later receive as his inheritance, obeyed and went, even though he did not *know where he was going. By **acting on a revelation** he made his home in the promised land like a stranger in a foreign country; he lived in tents, as did Isaac and Jacob, who were heirs with him of the same promise. For he was looking forward to the city with foundations, whose architect and builder is God. And by **acting on a revelation** even Sarah, who was past childbearing age, was enabled to bear children because she considered him faithful who had made the promise. And so from this one man, and he as good as dead, came descendants as numerous as the stars in the sky and as countless as the sand on the seashore.* HEBREWS 11:8-12

MOSES' PARENTS

*By **acting on a revelation** Moses' parents hid him for three months after he was born, because they saw he was no ordinary child, and they were not afraid of the king's edict.* HEBREWS 11:23

MOSES

*By **acting on a revelation** Moses, when he had grown up, refused to be known as the son of Pharaoh's daughter. He chose to be mistreated along with the people of God rather than to enjoy the fleeting pleasures of sin. He regarded disgrace for the sake of Christ as of greater value than the treasures of Egypt, because he was looking ahead to his reward. By **acting on a revelation** he left Egypt, not fearing the king's anger; he persevered because he saw him who is invisible. By **acting on a revelation** he kept the Passover and the application* *of blood, so that the destroyer of the firstborn would not touch the firstborn of*

Israel. HEBREWS 11:24-28

NATION OF ISRAEL

*By **acting on a revelation** the people passed through the Red Sea as on dry land; but when the Egyptians tried to do so, they were drowned. By **acting on a revelation** the walls of Jericho fell, after the army had marched around them for seven days.* HEBREWS 11:29

RAHAB

*By **acting on a revelation** the prostitute Rahab, because she welcomed the spies, was not killed with those who were disobedient.* HEBREWS 11:31

PRINCIPLES OF FAITH

If you were to study these stories from their Old Testament accounts, you would find that there are some constants, some life-changing principles that we can learn from.

First, each of these people had a revelation. God spoke to them. What was revealed to them brought them hope and confidence.

Did you notice how many times the word *see* or *saw* showed up in the quotes from Hebrews 11? These ancients instinctively knew that God was showing them things and speaking to them.

Second, others opposed them. Not everyone around these ancients had the same confidence. The reason most were in opposition was because they didn't see and hear what the ancients did. Some opposition was intense.

Third, miracles happened. God did amazing miracles for these ancients after they acted on revelation. He turned ideas into realities.

PROMISES RELATED TO FAITH

You will also find two life-transforming promises from God in Hebrews 11. The first comes from verse 6. It is all about **how to access God's pleasure and be rewarded for it**.

> And without faith it is impossible to **please God**, because anyone who comes to him must believe that he exists and that **he rewards** those who earnestly seek him. HEBREWS 11:6

The writer of this amazing book says that it is impossible to please God if we don't have faith. In other words, if we don't act on His revelations. *Impossible* is a strong term, but that is the word that's used. I want to please God. I want to put a smile on His face. I'm sure you do as well. We please Father God by acting on his revelations.

The second promise relates to **how God sees us and what he does for us**.

*Instead, they were longing for a better country—a heavenly one. Therefore, God is **not ashamed** to be called their God, for he **has prepared** a city for them.* HEBREWS 11:16

Did you know that God can be ashamed of us? I know this isn't a popular idea, but Hebrews definitely makes this a possibility. Apparently this is the dynamic that takes place when you and I don't act on His revelations. I don't want God to look at me negatively. I'm guessing neither do you. When we simply believe what God has revealed to us and have the confidence to act on his ideas, thoughts, dreams, etc., we move from shame to rewards. I like that.

Hebrews 11:6 says, *"He rewards those who earnestly seek him."* Hebrews 11:16 follows up with *"He has prepared a city for them."*

God loves it when we act on a revelation. He has good stuff in store for us as our reward—we enter the Faith Zone where miracles and breakthroughs are the norm.

REWARDS PREPARED FOR US

On one of our trips to the United Kingdom we experienced these principles first-hand. We were scheduled to leave on a Sunday night, but that morning we were at Catch The Fire Toronto listening to Patricia King preach. As part of her talk, she gave people the opportunity to sow into the ministry of Catch The Fire. She had asked us beforehand if she could do this.

As she was preaching I remembered (revelation) how she was going to conclude her talk. I got an offering envelope and began to prepare a gift (action). We were the first ones up to give our gift and within a few hours we were on a plane.

The next Sunday Sandra and I were speaking at an Elim Pentecostal church south of Liverpool. We got there early, while the band was setting up. A man I recognized came to greet me and asked if he could give me an offering. I thought that perhaps he was the treasurer of the church and this was my speaking gift. I responded positively. He asked if he could write the cheque on a Canadian account?

"Yes."

He came back a few minutes later and gave me a cheque for $300 Canadian.

I gave the cheque to Sandra because she handles our finances. She asked what this was. I said it was our speaking gift. Sandra said it couldn't be—another man had just given her our ministry gift. He had said that he was the church's financial officer.

Wow, we were blessed. Before the meeting had even started we received an extra gift.

In the meeting Sandra shared the story of how we received the money to purchase our home. The same man that blessed me came up at the end of the meeting. He asked if our mortgage was fully paid off. I said it wasn't. He asked if he could write a cheque for that? Affirmative.

He went away and came back with another cheque for $3000 towards our home! Sandra and I both recognized this as a reward for the offering we gave the previous Sunday.

Here is the best part: How is it possible that a man at a church in a small town in England had a Canadian bank account? How is it that he had more that $3000 in that account?

It is because God not only **rewards** us for faith steps but he also goes ahead of us and **prepares**. God had prepared a man in the UK to have a Canadian account with money in it before we arrived. I love this stuff!

I'd like to point out that this book is not all about money. Your reward for faith will not always be financial. Faith is not a get-rich-quick scheme. What I am saying is that God knows your needs, and if you act on the revelations he gives you, you will receive your reward. If your need is financial, you should expect a financial reward. If your need is for healing, you should expect a health-related reward. If your need is for favour, expect favour, and so on.

Your journey into the Faith Zone is part of the expansion of God's kingdom. When I look at what the ancients accomplished I see incredible things. Hebrews describes some of these astonishing rewards.

> *Who through faith* (acting on a revelation) *conquered kingdoms, administered justice, and gained what was promised; who shut the mouths of lions, quenched the fury of the flames, and escaped the edge of the sword; whose weakness was turned to strength; and who became powerful in battle and routed foreign armies. Women received back their dead, raised to life again.* **HEBREWS 11:33-35**

I want these rewards. I want to live in this zone now. I don't want to ever leave this realm. This zone is where the impossible is possible. This way of life has no boundaries, no walls. Nothing can stop the miraculous from happening.

Can it get any better? I'm not sure, but I'd like to try.

Will we get it right all the time? Probably not. Will our hope at times be more inspired by us than by God? Of course. Paul tells us that we don't always receive revelation clearly. *"For now we see only a reflection as in a mirror; then we shall see face to face. Now I know in part; then I shall know fully, even as I am fully known"*. (1 Corinthians 13:12)

There will be occasions when our actions aren't the action steps that the Lord intended. I get that. That is even more reason to step out and act on revelation. I need to learn how to respond to Him rather than doubting and not acting at all. If it is God speaking to me, there will be amazing results when I do my part. God will reward me in some way. I'll be in the Faith Zone. If the hope was rooted in myself and not in God, at least I tried and took a chance. I was attempting to live by faith. That too is good.

Will I see the results of my acting on revelation right away? Not necessarily. Some of the stories of the ancients show us that some breakthroughs take their time. Noah spent 120 years fulfilling his action: building an ark. The subsequent verses of Hebrews 11 tell us that many of the ancients didn't see their rewards in their lifetime. But that didn't stop them from acting on their revelations. The ancients believed that God had good stuff in store for them or for future generations.

SO HOW ABOUT US?

Does God communicate to us today? You bet.

Can we please God today? Yup. He wants us to.

Can we step out and try to live by faith? Well that is the big question.

The Bible has lots of people stories. I believe the reason for the biographies is to help us see how the principles of the Bible function. They are there to inspire us and stimulate our hope. In the next chapters we are going to look at accounts of people who interacted with Jesus. We are going to review historical stories, mostly from Matthew's account, of people who moved into the Faith Zone. I trust you will be inspired. My goal in writing this book is to help you enter the dimension of living I call the Faith Zone.

Here is a simple prayer as we conclude this chapter.

> *Father would you help us in this process. Would you please download*
> *ideas, concepts, and thoughts to us, your children? Help us not only*
> *to be hearers of your word, but doers as well. In Jesus' name, Amen.*

GOING DEEPER

1. Ask the Lord to remind you of the some of the dreams He has placed in your heart as a child or as an adult. Write down five of them.

2. Ask the Lord if any of them are still in play. If He says yes, ask Him what steps of action He would like you to take at this point in time to bring them forth.

ENDNOTES

[1]Eric David, *The Man Behind The Mouse* (retrieved December 2015) http://www.christianitytoday.com/ct/2009/novemberweb-only/fofdisney.html

[2]*Walt Disney Quotes* (retrieved December 2015) http://www.brainyquote.com/quotes/authors/w/walt_disney.html#P1lVcuHbmh4BXDlb.99

CHAPTER 2

Faith to Trust God for Provision

MATTHEW 6

Therefore, I tell you, do not worry about your life, what you will eat or drink; or about your body, what you will wear. Is not life more than food, and the body more than clothes? Look at the birds of the air; they do not sow or reap or store away in barns, and yet your heavenly Father feeds them. Are you not much more valuable than they? Can any one of you by worrying add a single hour to your life? And why do you worry about clothes? See how the flowers of the field grow. They do not labor or spin. Yet I tell you that not even Solomon in all his splendor was dressed like one of these. If that is how God clothes the grass of the field, which is here today and tomorrow is thrown into the fire, will he not much more clothe you—you of little faith? So do not worry, saying, 'What shall we eat?' or 'What shall we drink?' or 'What shall we wear?' For the pagans run after all these things, and your heavenly Father knows that you need them. But seek first his kingdom and his righteousness, and all these things will be given to you as well. Therefore do not worry about tomorrow, for tomorrow will worry about itself. Each day has enough trouble of its own.

MATTHEW 6:25–34

Trusting is a challenge. Trust is about both the process and the person. Do we have confidence in the systems that are in place? Do we believe the integrity of the person giving us the speech or telling us what to do? Is there a level of competency that allows us to trust the company or organization?

There is one who gets blamed all the time for all sorts of things. His name is God. Most people don't trust God. We pick and choose when and where to trust Him. Recently, one of the U.S. national newspapers asked if the "in God we trust" phrase should still be used on their currency. Eighty-six per cent said yes. Apparently people in the States feel they want to trust God.

Did you know that followers of Jesus don't trust God all of the time? We say we trust, but when it comes down to making decisions, often we don't have the ability or willingness to do so. We struggle to trust God to provide for us. We don't know if God will heal our bodies from sickness and diseases. We are unsure if God is able to find a spouse for us. The list goes on and on.

I believe this has been a battle since time began. The people of the Bible struggled over and over again to trust God. It is true for us today. In this chapter I'd like to rebuild your confidence in Father God.

LITTLE FAITH LEADS TO WORRY

Jesus knew people lacked trust in God. Jesus devoted a whole section of his most famous sermon to this topic. He answered key questions, such as can we trust God in general? Can we trust Him to provide for us? Will God be there when we need him?

One of Jesus' strongest negative statements in his sermon comes in Matthew 6:30. He said, *"you of little faith."*

Jesus said his listeners were not acting on the revelations that they had received from God. They were holding back. They were rarely able to enter the Faith Zone because they lacked trust. When Jesus tells his listeners not to worry, he leans on revelation that he believes they already have. Listen to how The Message translates this passage.

> *If you decide for God, living a life of God-worship, it follows that you don't fuss about what's on the table at mealtimes or whether the clothes in your closet are in fashion. There is far more to your life than the food you put in your stomach, more to your outer appearance than the clothes you hang on your body. Look at the birds, free and unfettered, not tied down to a job description, careless in the care of God. And you count far more to him than birds.*
> MATTHEW 6:25-26 THE MESSAGE

The key revelation is this: Does God care more for us or for birds? If God does care for us, then why do we worry? If God doesn't care about us, only then do we have the right to be stressed.

Jesus said more.

> *If God gives such attention to the appearance of wildflowers—most of which are never even seen—don't you think he'll attend to you, take pride in you, do*

his best for you? What I'm trying to do here is to get you to relax, to not be
so preoccupied with getting, so you can respond to God's giving. People who
don't know God and the way he works fuss over these things, but you know
both God and how he works. Steep your life in God-reality, God-initiative, and
God-provisions. Don't worry about missing out. You'll find all your everyday
human concerns will be met. MATTHEW 6:30–33, THE MESSAGE

Jesus was essentially asking, have you not had a personal revelation of
how God works? If you have, then why do you worry? If you haven't, then
you have the right to be preoccupied with the getting. People with *"little*
faith" are those who, in Jesus' estimation, have knowledge of how amazing
Father God is but aren't acting like it. They are looking after themselves
rather than focusing on others and on Him.

If Jesus had said his listeners had no faith, it would have meant that they
hadn't yet received any revelation of God's goodness. If God's revelation
brings hope, then no revelation means no hope. No hope means there is
nothing to act on, which results in no faith. But Jesus didn't say no faith.
He said little faith. Because the people did know Father God, because
they did know the principles that God wants us to live by, they were held
accountable. You and I fall into this category.

"Pagans" (Matthew 6:32) are not held accountable because they don't yet
know God. But as a devoted follower of Jesus, I need to be acting on what
I know, fully confident that when I do, God will provide for me.

Jesus simply and succinctly reminds us of God's principles in this sermon
on the mountain. He hoped that his listeners would receive a revelation

that God is good. He is speaking to us today as well. Here is His key statement: *"But seek first his kingdom and his righteousness, and all these things will be given to you as well"* (Matthew 6:33). Followers of Jesus seek God's kingdom instead of their own. We follow our Father's code of conduct instead of our own. As we do this, our heavenly Father takes care of everything else.

Perhaps three of the most outstanding miracles Jesus performed are related to food. Jesus turned water to wine, and twice he fed thousands of people. These miracles model the extravagance of God, that He can provide for us anywhere and any time.

THE WEDDING IN CANA

Ken Gott[1] has a great sermon from John 2. This is the story of a wedding where the wine was about to run out. Water was used to make wine. Ken's point is simple; God takes what we have and multiplies it. Ken said that this wedding was going to be known as the wedding reception where they ran out of wine, but because Jesus was at the reception, it became known as the wedding where each guest took home a case of extraordinary wine.

The six water pots should equal about eight hundred bottles of wine. Most bottles of wine give five to six glasses. So, let's do some math: I think we can safely assume it was a small reception; Cana was a small town. Perhaps a hundred people lived there. The twelve uninvited guests Jesus brought apparently caused the wine shortage, so that gives us an idea how many were invited to the reception. If everyone had already had at least one glass, perhaps two, and if they were all going to have one more glass to finish the night off, then that means that Jesus made enough wine to serve 4,000 to 4,800 people. These are Faith Zone numbers.

God is extravagant. He is able to do more than we can ask, imagine, or think (Ephesians 3:20).

THE DAY AWAY IN GALILEE

That same principle of extravagance is seen when thousands of people took the day off work and went to a meeting with Jesus in the hills of Galilee.

The accounts of the first fish and bread story tell us five thousand men were present plus their wives and kids (Matthew 14:21). The second time Jesus fed a crowd, four thousand men were present, plus women and children (Matthew 15:38). If by men Matthew means married men, then there is a good chance that five thousand married women were also present. So how many kids were there?

If you have been to Israel and been in the Orthodox area of Jerusalem, you will know that there are lots of kids. These folks have huge families. Our tour guide told us that some couples have up to 20 children. In New York City, the average number of children in Hasidic and Haredi families is 6.72.[2] The average is the very same in Jerusalem.[3] Orthodox Jews in Israel today have one of the highest averages of children in our world. I'm guessing families were larger in Jesus' day.

Okay, let's finish the math. If 6.7 is the number today and there were 5,000 couples, this brings us to 33,500 children. A grand total of 43,500 people got at least one free fish sandwich that day. If everyone ate two sandwiches, we are getting close to 100,000 meals. These are Faith Zone numbers.

Everyone was fed well. They had leftovers. I'm sure that news of this miracle and the subsequent feeding of 36,800 spread around the nation. Get the picture? Jesus' disciples should know this truth; they've been a part of all three miracles.

SOMEONE FORGOT TO BRING LUNCH

Can we trust God to provide for us? Let me share another story that relates to trusting God for provision.

One day Jesus was with his Twelve.[4] They were crossing the Sea of Galilee and something interesting happened on the boat ride. *"When they went across the lake, the disciples forgot to take bread"* (Matthew 16:5). If I were one of the Twelve I would be thinking, who didn't get the memo that it was their turn to bring a bag lunch for everyone? Perhaps they all knew who it was. We'll find out the answer to this very important question when we get to heaven. Jesus made a very blunt statement to them. *"'Be careful,' Jesus said to them. 'Be on your guard against the yeast of the Pharisees and Sadducees'"* (Matthew 16:6).

The reaction of the Twelve, the men who are being trained as the leaders of The Way,[5] is classic: *"They discussed this among themselves and said, 'It is because we didn't bring any bread'"* (Matthew 16:7).

Let's review. These disciples were all at the wedding in Cana (John 2:2). Not only were they with Jesus at the two free fish fillet meals, but they were the ones doing the miracle and serving the food! I'll talk about that point in a moment. Now, a few weeks or months later, they were muttering in a boat about who forgot to bring lunch.

How is this possible? How can they not be at a place of complete confidence that God can provide for them at any time? That is the precise question we need to ask of ourselves.

Guess what Jesus said to them?

> Aware of their discussion, Jesus asked, "You of little faith, why are you talking among yourselves about having no bread? Do you still not understand? Don't you remember the five loaves for the five thousand, and how many basketfuls you gathered? Or the seven loaves for the four thousand, and how many basketfuls you gathered? MATTHEW 16:8-10

He tells them they have "*little faith.*"
Do you see the other phrases of Jesus?

> "*Do you still not understand? Don't you remember the five loaves for the five thousand?*"

What Jesus questioned was their faith process. Did the wedding and the two free picnics not give them the revelation that provision would never be a problem? If they had a revelation that Jesus could look after them, then their actions should have been based on a provision reality. Sadly, they had very limited confidence. They talked openly about who was to blame. They were acting and talking as if they had no confidence and no hope. They were not in the Faith Zone.

Before we laugh at them, we need to understand that this is how we are. Well, at least it is how I am. I'm constantly second guessing how God will provide for me. I know He has in the past, but will He do it again?

So when there is a special mission's offering, or I know of a family in lack, I need to act based on what I know about God, not based on how much money I have in my pocket.

When I'm the one on the stage at our church in Toronto and leading the offering segment, I want people to hear God, so that they can act accordingly. When I am in the seats and an appeal to be generous is given by someone else, this is my challenge. Will I be generous knowing that God is my provider? I get a dollar number and I think, *What? There's no way I can afford that.* I look in my wallet and base my generosity on what I have with me, not on what I heard God say.

The words of Jesus should be ringing in my head. *Steve of little faith.*

LISTENING FOR AN OFFERING

On one of my better hearing days I was at Newmarket Alliance church, about 70 kilometers (40 miles) north of Toronto. We were there to learn from a healing specialist. We got to the church building early and found that the doors were still locked. So we went to a hamburger restaurant across the street for a quick meal.

While eating my burger the Lord spoke to me.
"Are you planning to give an offering tonight?"
"Now that you mention it, yes."

I had no cash with me so I went to an ATM and took out $30, which was the amount I thought I heard to give. We ate and went to the meeting. Sandra and I were seated in the middle, a few seats back from the front row. A great place to watch a healer do the stuff.

At the end of the night I realized that they hadn't taken an offering. I knew one of the leaders and so I asked if this was an oversight. I told him that I had taken one of their offering envelopes and had my $30 ready. Could he take it? Kurt went to talk to the pastor to see if they had missed the offering. While he was inquiring, the Lord spoke to me again.

"Do you really want to give tonight?"
"Yup."
"Okay, add another zero to the gift."

Ahhhh, okay. An opportunity to enter the Faith Zone.

Kurt returned and told me they hadn't planned to take an offering for the speaker, but yes I could give my $30. I now had a problem as I needed to give $300. I asked how I could do that. He wasn't sure, as they didn't take credit cards payments. I told him that I would mail a cheque, which I did the following day. I acted on the revelation, the thoughts that I'd received from the Lord. God had spoken to me twice about giving, in the burger place and at the church. He even told me the exact amounts. I acted with confidence knowing I was obeying the direction of the Lord.

The backstory is that I was getting ready to go to Oasis Church, an amazing multicultural congregation in the Wimbledon area of London, England. I was going there to teach our Encounter course. Teaching the twelve talks over a Friday and Saturday is very tiring. I had wanted to take another person with me but I didn't have the funds.

Remember in the first chapter I explained how God rewards people who act on his revelations? Well that very week as my cheque was in the mail to Newmarket, I got a cheque in the mail from Oasis. They had decided to send me a speaking gift prior to my arrival. Wow, that rarely happens. The amount of the cheque was exactly enough for two plane tickets to London, England. I took Bruno Ierullo with me, who just happens to now pastor a Catch The Fire church in... Newmarket! How cool is that?

Twice I heard the Lord ask me to give. First $30 and then $300. I believe that because I gave that money away, the Lord rewarded me. How did He do this? He was working behind the scenes to make preparations for me. Father God prompted a church in London to bless me prior to going there.

This is how faith works. We listen, we act, and we get in the Faith Zone. He rewards those who live by faith.

MIRACLES HAPPEN IN OUR HANDS

Let's go back to the disciples in the boat who were muttering about lunch. How is it possible for them to have forgotten so quickly that provision is not a problem for God? If you read the fine print in the stories of the fish fillets, you will see that Jesus didn't do the multiplying of the fish and bread. It was the disciples. He took the initial 5 loaves and 2 fish and divided them among the Twelve. Then He tasked them to put people in groups of 50 and 100 and to go and feed them.

Imagine this challenge.

James chooses a group of 50. All he has in his hand is part of a fish and a bit of bread. He's thinking, *good luck on this one if something miraculous doesn't happen.* These people are all hungry. There could be a riot. He breaks the fish head in half and gives it to a child. The child smiles, as do the mom and dad. James looks back in his hand to get some bread and notices that the whole fish head is still there. What...?

He takes some of the bread and gives it away. It reappears. *Let's try this again*, he thinks. He moves to the mom. He gives her almost all of the fish and almost all of the bread. In a flash, he has everything he just gave away.

This is how the miracle took place. With great excitement they would have been moving around the hills serving fish sandwiches. If 43,500 people were in attendance, that means that each disciple served 3,625 people. And there were leftovers.

So, let's recreate the thought process of these Twelve disciples who are now in a boat with no lunch. Why were they talking about who forgot to bring lunch? Early in their ministry they had gone home with a case of fine wine courtesy of newlyweds in Cana. Twice in the last few months they had leftover fish sandwiches to take to their families. Now they are wondering how they will get lunch. Little faith would be the correct way to label them.

Little faith is better than no faith though. No faith means that I haven't done anything at all with any of the revelations God has given me. Little faith means that I've perhaps given it a thought, perhaps pondered doing something, but I didn't. The challenge that each of us face continuously is to remember the goodness of God. Some of us don't yet have personal stories of God's provision. That is one of the reasons why we are to be attending a church and being in community, so we can hear the stories of others and receive encouragement.

One of the reasons the revival meetings at Catch The Fire Toronto lasted for twelve years is because it was testimony-driven. Almost every night we had upwards of three to five people sharing what God had done the night before. People would go home and tell their church, their friends, their family what happened to them, or what they had seen and heard. We'd see them back again but this time with someone else. Testimonies were our Facebook.

The stories in the Bible are written to give us hope. When we read what God did for people in the past, we can have confidence that he can do the same for us today. If Jesus is the same yesterday, today, and forever, then miracles can still happen (Hebrews 13:8). God is still able to care for me.

God can provide for me. I need to bank this truth for the day when I need to move into the Faith Zone. I need to be able to reach into my account and draw out confidence. Because of this hope I can act with confidence and assurance. When I do act, I put myself into a place where God takes over. He becomes my rewarder.

I like that place. I hope you do too.

I trust that my insights into the Scriptures and my personal stories are becoming part of your revelatory DNA. My desire is that you will never again wonder if you can trust God.

SECRETS TO GOD'S PROVISION

God can help us when we are struggling with what to do. In fact, in the passage we began with, Father God gives us precise instructions. Our part, according to Jesus in Matthew 6, is threefold:

First, I am not to worry, but to be full of hope and confidence. God looks after birds and flowers. I'm better than they are. Of course He cares for me.

Second, I am to seek His kingdom. I am to be putting God first in every area of my life. The quick test to know if we are living this way is to ask ourselves some questions: Does God get our time? Does He get His tithe? Does He get our heart?

If we cannot answer yes to these questions, there are no guarantees from

God. He isn't obligated to keep His side of the equation if you are not keeping yours. His promise on this topic is very conditional.

Third, I am to live a righteous life. Am I living like Jesus? Am I acting like Jesus? Do people think I look like Jesus?

There are 99 different negative attitudes, character traits, and lifestyles that the New Testament details. Followers of Jesus are to be getting rid of all 99 of them. Instead, we are to be putting on all the good things that come through a relationship with Jesus and a dependence on the Holy Spirit. If you are living by these three kingdom principles, you have no need to worry. God will be speaking to you with more revelation. If you do what He says with confidence and speed, a reward is waiting for you.

Let me pray for you.

> *Father, would you please help us to live by these three simple principles. Would you enable us to hear you over and over again? Please speak to our spirit so that we can know what to do and when to do it. We want to hear you, we want to obey you, and we want to trust you. We want to live in the Faith Zone. In the name of Jesus, Amen.*

GOING DEEPER

1. Ask the Lord to remind you of a time when you didn't trust him about your finances. Ask the Lord to fill in the blanks for you. What did I miss? Why didn't I trust?

2. Was there a time I did trust and things went awry? Lord, what did I miss then? Are there past experiences I simply need to set aside and choose to simply trust God even though I do not understand?

3. What is a current financial challenge that you face? Ask the Lord for an insight into what He wants to do. Ask the Lord what you need to do to make it happen.

ENDNOTES

[1] Ken Gott, bethshanchurch.net

[2] Wikipedia, *Borough Park, Brooklyn* (retrieved December 2015) http://en.wikipedia.org/wiki/Borough_Park,_Brooklyn

[3] Gershom Gorenberg, *An Orthodox Challenge* (retrieved December 2015) http://www.prospectmagazine.co.uk/magazine/an-orthodox-challenge-gershom-gorenberg-israel-jerusalem-jews/#.U4T6Ff0QRuY

[4] Twelve—I am choosing to use the term Twelve rather than "disciples." The group is often described as the Twelve (Matthew 10:1-2), and I am trying to distinguish this group from the larger group of disciples that Jesus had. For example, John 6:66 tells us that many disciples left Jesus when he began to talk about drinking his blood.

[5] The Way was the name of the church in Jerusalem. It was based on the statement that Jesus was The Way (Acts 9:2).

CHAPTER 3

A Centurion's Great Faith

MATTHEW 8

When Jesus had entered Capernaum, a centurion came to him, asking for help. "Lord," he said, "my servant lies at home paralyzed, suffering terribly." Jesus said to him, "Shall I come and heal him?" The centurion replied, "Lord, I do not deserve to have you come under my roof. But just say the word, and my servant will be healed. For I myself am a man under authority, with soldiers under me. I tell this one, 'Go,' and he goes; and that one, 'Come,' and he comes. I say to my servant, 'Do this,' and he does it." When Jesus heard this, he was amazed and said to those following him, "Truly I tell you, I have not found anyone in Israel with such great faith. I say to you that many will come from the east and the west, and will take their places at the feast with Abraham, Isaac and Jacob in the kingdom of heaven. But the subjects of the kingdom will be thrown outside, into the darkness, where there will be weeping and gnashing of teeth." Then Jesus said to the centurion, "Go. Let it be done just as you believed it would." And his servant was healed at that moment. **MATTHEW 8:5-13**

Everyone needs to visit Capernaum. The ruins of the city are a must for every tour group in Israel. It is one of my favourite places to visit because of the rich history of the town. My guess is that there were about 75 homes in this ancient town. The streets were narrow and the homes very small. Most homes would fit into your bathroom.

This is also the city where Jesus' best miracles took place. The synagogue where Jesus did his first deliverance is still there (Mark 1:21–28). You can walk on the floors, touch the walls, and still sense God's presence. Jesus would have stood on those steps many times. Peter's home, where Jesus went on the Sabbath and ministered to Peter's mother-in-law, is right down the street (Mark 1:29–31). It is less than a thirty-second walk.

The first large-scale revival meeting, where Jesus healed everyone who came, was in this town (Luke 4:38–41). This meeting was probably held in the market area, which is adjacent to Peter's home and the synagogue. The mayor of Capernaum had his son healed when he tracked Jesus down a few days' journey away in Cana (John 4:46–54). He was called a royal official, possibly meaning that he might be related to Herod the Great.

Jairus, the chairman of the synagogue board of directors, had his daughter raised from the dead in this very town (Matthew 9:18–26). The lame man, whose four friends got him into a closed meeting through the roof, was healed in Capernaum (Matthew 9:1–8). A lady who had her menstrual period non-stop for twelve years was healed in this town (Matthew 9:20–22). Two blind men and a mute man invaded a home in Capernaum; they went into the home where Jesus was resting and got their miracles (Matthew 9:27–34).

Jesus also lived here. I'll have much more on this topic in later chapters.

Capernaum was used to great miracles, healings, and deliverances. The people knew that when Jesus showed up great things would happen. They had faith.

THE ROMAN CENTURION

The majority of the chapters in this book tells those stories. One miracle in Capernaum stands out to me for several reasons: the healing of the Roman Centurion's servant. Why?

First, because it happens with another key city official; the centurion was in essence the chief of police. The mayor and synagogue ruler, the other big wigs in town, had already had great encounters with Jesus.

Second, this Gentile is the first man to figure out the key to Jesus' healing powers. We'll look at what his revelation was and how he acted on it. He gets into the Faith Zone and receives an amazing miracle.

A Roman centurion would have been the commander of about 80 soldiers. My guess is that he was stationed in Capernaum with only a few soldiers. Most of his men would be spread over the region. His job was to keep the peace on behalf of Rome in northern Galilee. The passage tells us that he had a servant. This would probably be a young Jewish boy; I'm guessing less than thirteen. If the centurion had a servant, it means that he was a person of wealth who could afford the help. (If the boy was conscripted, he would be called a slave rather than servant.) Someone of the centurion's significance would be well known, especially because Capernaum was a small town with a population of about a thousand people. Everyone would know who this Roman centurion was.

Let me walk you through this amazing story as I see it. By the way, I like to imagine the narratives. So please forgive me for embellishing and adding my thoughts to what happened. My insights are not divine, but hopefully inspiring.

Jesus enters the city, probably from the western side of the town. The main street runs between Peter's home on the southwest corner of the town and the synagogue on the northwest corner. Peter was one of the rich guys in town. Archeologists have found Peter's home and conveniently there is now a marvelous Catholic church with a glass floor built over it. His home was quite a bit bigger than most of the homes in Capernaum, which is how we know he was wealthy.

As Jesus comes into the city, the centurion greets him and asks for help. The help that he needs is not personal, it is for his servant. From reading into the text I am going to assume that something tragic has recently happened to his young servant. I doubt that a person of significance such as this Roman legionnaire would hire a paralyzed servant. Rather, he would have hired someone who can handle the physical work.

"My servant lies at home paralyzed, suffering terribly" (Matthew 8:6). Something has happened, an accident or perhaps an illness, that has caused this young man to need a miracle. The boy's suffering is described as terrible.

You know how some people don't let you finish a sentence? I'm like that.

Sandra will say something and I jump in assuming that I already know the rest of the conversation. Usually I am wrong. Jesus did this too. He assumes that he is about to be asked to go to the centurion's home to heal the boy, so he says it, *"Shall I come and heal him?"* (Matthew 8:7).

WHAT DID THE ROMAN KNOW?

What comes next is a mind-blowing statement of faith. In fact, Jesus would then comment to this Roman and to all who were listening that he had never heard this kind of declaration before from a Jew or a Gentile. Not even Jesus' own disciples had exhibited such great faith. What did the man say to cause Jesus to make this kind of statement?

Let's keep reading the text.

> The centurion replied, "Lord, I do not deserve to have you come under my roof. But just say the word, and my servant will be healed. For I myself am a man under authority, with soldiers under me. I tell this one, 'Go,' and he goes; and that one, 'Come,' and he comes. I say to my servant, 'Do this,' and he does it."
> MATTHEW 8:8-9

In these two sentences we have the key to what great faith is. Did you see it?

As soon as the Roman soldier said these words, we have this awesome pronouncement from Jesus about great faith, great acting on revelation.

When Jesus heard this, he was amazed and said to those following him,
"Truly I tell you, I have not found anyone in Israel with such great faith."
MATTHEW 8:10

Before I share the officer's revelation, let's back up and review how faith works. I want you to grasp the process so you begin to see it in the Scriptures and practice it in your own life.

Faith starts with a revelation that causes hope to flourish. An idea, a thought, a possibility. We call that hope. If we do something because of the hope, this revelation we've received, that action is called faith (Hebrews 11:1). We know what the action statement of the centurion is. He told Jesus that he doesn't need to come to the home; he simply needs to command the miraculous healing.

Amazing. But what was his revelation? What was it that this Roman knew that even Jesus' own disciples didn't know? When I teach on this passage I often ask people this very question. People respond with many good comments.

The soldier understood authority. Yes.
The soldier knew that Jesus could heal. Yes.
The soldier humbled himself and declared his need. Yes.

All of these are right, but they are not the big one. Are you ready for it? In Matthew 8:9 we hear his revelation: *"For I myself am a man under authority."* This Roman had figured out that Jesus was not the one healing people. Jesus was the middleman. It was someone of greater authority than Jesus who is doing the healing, Jesus was simply the mouth and the hands. Jesus is the middleman.

Wow. Did you grasp this truth?

JESUS IS UNDER AUTHORITY

Jesus, as the divine son of God, wasn't healing people in and of himself. Jesus was *"under authority"* just like this Roman centurion was. Because he was a soldier he understood the concept of chain of command. As a military man he knew that when an order was given in Rome, it got passed down the ranks to people like himself. He in turn ordered his men to do what was commissioned by the higher-ups. This chief of police from Capernaum was the very first person in the history of the world to figure out that Jesus was simply following orders from heaven. Wow.

Do you remember my story about the offering while visiting a church in Newmarket, Ontario? I was there to hear a healing specialist, Roger Sapp.[1] Roger is the one I first heard share this insight. When I heard him, it rocked my world. Literally overnight, my ability to heal the sick jumped up several levels. If Jesus, a man under authority, was getting revelation and simply acting on it, well, I could do that too! I can receive insights from the Lord. I can act on them. I can also exhibit great faith. I can enter the Faith Zone.

This soldier could have agreed with Jesus and said something like, "Yes, come to my home and heal my servant." I'm sure that the boy would have been healed and everyone would have been in awe. But because he had a revelation that was greater than everyone else's, he was able to say something that set him apart. His statement to Jesus, *"Just say the word, and my servant will be healed,"* puts this man in the great faith category.

There is only one other person in all of the Scriptures that is recorded to have had great faith. We will look at her story in a later chapter.

GREAT FAITH KNOWS THINGS OTHERS DON'T KNOW

Great faith knows that you don't need Jesus to lay his hands on your servant for a healing.
Great faith knows that Jesus doesn't have to say a fancy prayer for the sick to recover.
Great faith knows that Jesus doesn't have to be physically present for a miracle to happen.
Great faith knows that a simple command from Jesus is a powerful command from heaven.
Great faith knows that I can also do this kind of stuff.
Great faith knows that all obstacles can be overcome in the Faith Zone.

I can heal the sick, I can do miracles, and I can raise the dead. Not because of me, but because of whom my Father is. Wow.

My Father talks to me.
My Father gives me insights.
My Father directs me.
My Father allows his Spirit to reside in me.

My role is to act on what I know and have confidence that God will do the rest.

My role is to demonstrate to God and the world how easy faith is; faith is acting on a revelation.

Matthew 8:10 says that Jesus was *"amazed."* Can you picture the surprise on Jesus' face when he hears the centurion's faith statement? I can imagine Jesus' eyes opening, a huge grin on his face, his hands raised in shock and praise.

Jesus turns with his head nodding and looks at his Twelve. He looks at the crowd of people from Capernaum. He looks to see if they've just understood what was just said. Did they hear what Jesus heard? Jesus is hopeful that everyone else has just caught this revelation as well.

But, sadly, no. Jesus was the only one with ears to hear.

A COMMENDATION AND A REBUKE

Because no one else got the revelation, Jesus utilized the opportunity to teach the good people of Capernaum. He commended the centurion and rebuked everyone else.

> *"Truly I tell you, I have not found anyone in Israel with such great faith. I say to you that many will come from the east and the west, and will take their places at the feast with Abraham, Isaac and Jacob in the kingdom of heaven. But the subjects of the kingdom will be thrown outside, into the darkness, where there will be weeping and gnashing of teeth."* **MATTHEW 8:10-12**

The commendation is that this man has more faith than anyone Jesus has previously met in all of Israel. That is quite the statement. This public blessing is also a position statement—Jesus was praising a Gentile. Jesus then directed his words to the town and the Twelve. Just because they were Jewish does not give them an automatic entry into the kingdom of heaven. He said many of them would miss heaven and end up in darkness.

Interesting. Hearing the great faith statement of the centurion really shook Jesus up. I'm quite sure that when the people gathered to meet Jesus earlier that morning they didn't expect to be told off.

GO

After Jesus rebukes the crowd, he turns his attention back to the soldier.

> Then Jesus said to the centurion, "Go. Let it be done just as you believed it
> would." And his servant was healed at that moment. MATTHEW 8:13

Amazing. The centurion began his request by asking Jesus to *"just say the word"* (Matthew 8:8). That is precisely what Jesus does: *"Go"* (Matthew 8:13).

One word.
One command is all it took for the servant to be instantly healed. The servant boy wasn't even there. The boy may have known that his master was going to ask Jesus for help. The boy's mom and dad may even have been with the Roman officer when he made his request. We don't know.

A question for you: did the people in Capernaum know how Jesus would respond to the chief of police? They would be hopeful that the boy would be healed based on prior experiences. However, an instant healing without the boy present was way past their expectations. They were probably very expectant that Jesus would be convinced to come to the parent's home, to see the boy in his terrible state, to have compassion on him, to say something, to perhaps touch him. Then a miracle would take place.

No one expected this. A simple *"Go"* from Jesus.

The centurion may have been just as shocked as everyone else. Perhaps this great revelation came to him as he was approaching Jesus. It is possible that God dropped the thought in his heart right then and there. However the revelation came, this man takes the next step required for entry into the Faith Zone. He does something; he acts based on the revelatory thought. He courageously tells Jesus to speak the command, and Jesus responds in the affirmative. Soldiers are accustomed to commands. The centurion would have received them and given them. Jesus seems to have a knack for connecting with the people he meets, to be able to speak their language. So a simple military style command is given. *"Go."*

WHAT DID THE SOLDIER BELIEVE?

Did you note the final statement of Jesus to the centurion? Let's look at it again. *"'Go. Let it be done just as you believed it would.' And his servant was healed at that moment"* (Matthew 8:13).

Remember how we talked about the Faith Zone principle that God rewards people who act in faith. The healing of a severely paralyzed youth happens because the centurion *"believed it would."* Jesus is affirming the faith process. He is telling this soldier, you got it. You understand how faith works, well done.

So, what did the centurion believe?

That Jesus didn't need to be at the boy's side for the healing to take place. That Jesus wasn't doing the actual healing; it was a loving Father in heaven. That if Jesus gave one simple command, one word, it would be done.

What did the centurion receive as his reward?

Everything he believed for. He got a great healing for his young servant because he acted on his great revelation.

FAITH FOR WORLD CUP TICKETS

In June of 2014 I was able to attend a World Cup football (soccer) match in Brazil. The process of this adventure started in 2012 as an idea. Because it was related to sports, I took it as a God-thought. I love sports and competition, so when the idea dropped into my spirit to see a game live, it had to be God. I talked to Anderson Lima, the lead pastor of Catch The Fire Novo Hamburgo, our first church plant in Brazil. I asked him what he thought about the two of us organizing a pastor's conference around the same dates as the World Cup.

He agreed and we began to plan. This was two years out.

Partners in Harvest (PIH) is the global network of churches that our church in Toronto is a part of. I was at the European gathering of PIH pastors in the spring of 2012 when this thought came. Anderson was also there. We talked to all our football loving European pastor friends. All sorts of them thought this would be a great ministry trip.

I later sent a Facebook message to all the PIH leaders and asked who was in. I got about 25 responses. Most of them asking if I already had tickets. No, tickets were not on sale until the spring of 2014. We didn't even know which countries were playing yet.

Slowly the pastors began to drop out for a variety of reasons. Most wanted an assurance that I would be able to get tickets before they committed to purchasing airfares. I had no assurances other than the idea that the Lord gave me. Apparently that wasn't good enough.

Five of us were in as of January 2014. Sadly, two had to drop out for good reasons. Rick D'Orazio, who leads Freedom Centre in Oakville, had a heart attack and was ordered to stay calm during his recovery. He is a crazy Italian so calm is not possible if he is watching soccer. Gilberto Lima, a Brazilian now living in Toronto, was my main hope to get tickets. Gilberto personally knows former influential and famous Brazilian football players. He wasn't able to get tickets from any from them. Sadly, he had a death in the family and used up his holiday time because of that. So he couldn't come either.

So, there were just three of us. Bruno Ierullo is another crazy Italian football lover. Anderson Lima, living in Brazil, was the other one. My English heritage dictates that I'm also a football fanatic. My grandfather was involved with Leicester City Football club years ago. Most of the club worked for my grandfather during the war and played football on Saturdays. I spend most Saturday mornings watching my favourite team—Arsenal.

Bruno and I both decided that we would purchase our flights despite not yet having World Cup tickets. FIFA, the governing body that distributes the tickets, had several lotteries. Anderson, Bruno, and I had put our names in the hat but had heard nothing so far. Six weeks before the first match, Bruno and I got a text from Anderson to say that he had three tickets for us. Yes, God! Our acting on the revelation was rewarded. Those who wanted to see the tickets in hand before they made their travel plans had no reward. We were in the Faith Zone.

REWARD NUMBER ONE

Bruno left a few days before me. I was supposed to fly on a Sunday night from Toronto to Porto Allegre via Atlanta and Brasilia. The leaders conference would begin on the Tuesday morning.

When I arrived at Pearson Airport in Toronto I was told that I was being put on a flight to New York because the Atlanta flight had mechanical problems. They would reroute me through Sao Paulo. Fine, it would mean getting into Porto Allegre 90 minutes later. As we were about to board the New York flight, I noticed several people rushing the departure desk. Their smart phones had just alerted them that New York's JFK airport was locking out flights and ours was one of them.

I got in line too. They rescheduled me for a later flight to Atlanta thinking I may just make my connection. Ninety minutes later, that plane too had mechanical problems and was delayed. I went back to the counter and the Delta agent calmly overrode the system and put me back on the New York flight. It had finally been granted permission to leave Toronto. Because of the large volume of flights in and out of JFK airport, the Sao Paulo plane was also being delayed. I would have a chance to make it.

I was the last one to board the plane. Within a minute of being seated, the pilot came into the cabin and took the microphone. He said that New York had just told them that our flight was going to be delayed an additional hour. We were back on the hold list. Because this was an air traffic control issue, Delta would not be compensating anyone who missed his or her connection. He pointed out that we had two options if we had connecting flights.

Hotels and meal would be at our expense. So, our two options were staying on the plane and paying all costs at our connection point, or deplane, stay in Toronto, and book for the next day. I felt the Lord whisper to me to "start the journey." I stayed on the plane. I didn't know it, but I had just stepped into a Faith Zone.

A few folks made a different choice and quietly got off the plane. I travel a lot and the norm when a flight is delayed is lots of grumbling from the passengers. But this flight was different; the mood was good. The two flight attendants were joking and the pilot was doing his best to answer scenario questions. The amazing Delta gate agent that had helped me rebook three times came onto the plane with boxes of donuts. He walked down the aisle and served us warm, sugar-coated treats. I've never seen this before. We were all very happy. One of the men on the plane was a blind jazz musician going to a gig in New York. He took out his harmonica and entertained us as we waited. Everyone was happy. Everyone was talking to the people seated beside them, including me.

By the time we arrived in New York I had missed my Sao Paulo connection by 30 minutes. At the customer service desk many travelers tried to reschedule their missed flights. The process was taking a long time because a single ticket agent manned the desk. As I explained my series of bookings, the agent asked to see my original ticket to Atlanta.

Because my original flight had had mechanical problems, I was considered a guest of Delta. She provided me a free hotel room, free food vouchers, and free taxi vouchers. Rewards for listening and doing! I was happy to know that my Father was looking after me. Faith Zone rewards were kicking in.

REWARD NUMBER TWO

I got to my hotel, the Garden Inn, about midnight. I watched a bit of the news and was in bed before one a.m. What happened next I now believe was another reward for listening and staying on the flight to New York.

During the night I either had a dream or I was in a vision like the Apostle Paul talked about in 2 Corinthians 12. I'm not sure what it was, but it was real. I was standing outside an ancient revival church in the Niagara region of Canada. The Holy Spirit landed on me and I was out, lying on the grass, enjoying His presence. Almost at once, three revivalists, whom I know, were with me. They were also overwhelmed by the Holy Spirit and lay on the grass.

Marc Dupont is one of the prophets that spoke the Toronto Blessing into being. Jim Paul, a church planter, prophet and revivalist, from Hamilton, Ontario, was there. Mark Rudner was also present. Mark leads a revival church near Ottawa, Ontario, and recently led a series of meetings west of Toronto that lasted several months.

Suddenly, hundreds of people also seeking revival were with us. We were all incapacitated. I tried to text, call, and email John Arnott my pastor. I couldn't get my mind around how to do it. I was simply too overwhelmed. Several times during the night I woke up shaking. Power was surging through my body. I would go back into the dream/vision and it would start again.

At one point in the vision, the three revivalists and I were able to function a bit better. As we stood discussing what to make of our experience, a horrific accident happened on the street right in front of us. Two cars collided head on and the driver of one was thrown out the windshield. He went quite high and landed on his back directly opposite us on the other side of the street. Broken glass fell from the sky and cut his body open.

It looked to me as if his back had been snapped when he landed. He wasn't dead but probably he was only just alive. His body was severely lacerated. He would surely die within minutes. At that very instant emergency service vehicles arrived. Fire, ambulance, and police were all there ready to assist. The EMS people began to gather their equipment to rush to the man's aid.

Instinctively I moved to help. But before I could even take one step the Lord sovereignly healed the dying man. He jumped to his feet, shook off the glass fragments and said, "I'm good."

The EMS all knew that the man didn't need attention anymore. So instead of assisting the man they gathered in a huddle to talk and joke around. Our group of revivalists also did the same. We were marvelling at what God had just done. I then heard the Lord say to me, "Soon and very soon."

I woke up right at six a.m. I was still shaking. Electricity flowed through my body as I walked to the toilet trying to process what had happened. I didn't recall having an experience like it ever before. I believe God gave me that experience as a reward for listening to a simple revelation: "Start the journey."

Father God gave me a wonderful experience in room 213 for staying on a plane despite some challenges and possible financial obstacles. I was thinking as I was sitting on the plane at the gate in Toronto that this was going to cost me a hotel room, taxi fares, and meals, and I would miss a day in Brazil. As it turned out, Delta covered all my costs.

REWARD NUMBER THREE

The rewards kept coming. I got the overnight flight Monday evening from JFK to Sao Paulo. When I arrived in Brazil my luggage didn't. Delta gave me another $50 voucher. I purchased my ticket with Visa, which has a great travel benefit that gives me $1000 for a delayed flight. I got to spend some money on nice clothes. Rewards for acting on revelations.

There is more to this story.

As I wrote that last segment, I was sitting at the gate in Sao Paulo waiting for my next flight. Because I had five hours to wait, I started rewriting parts of this book. I added that story.

About twenty minutes before my fight I heard an announcement and the words *Porto Allegre*. I saw people stand up and move about and since I don't speak Portuguese I assumed it was a pre-boarding announcement. It wasn't. My gate had changed. By the time I figured it out I was too late. I ran past the security counter of the new gate and onto the jet way just as it was being pulled away.

Frustrated at myself, I was directed back to the agents. One gal who spoke good English took an hour of her time to help me. She took me to five different counters before we found the right one—Delta. The guys at the counter looked at my travel record and laughed. They laughed again when I told them that I had missed my flight despite sitting at the gate for five hours.

So as I write this, I am now at a different gate, waiting to see what comes next. Oh, by the way, the Delta agents gave me another voucher for a nice buffet meal. Still getting rewarded!

SPEAKING OUT OUR FAITH STATEMENTS

Back to Matthew's account of great faith in Capernaum. This miracle of the servant boy could have been just another wonderful healing story in Capernaum. But because of one man's great faith, it became a spectacular story. This healing is the testimony of how one man's faith can change a whole town.

The key in this story is that this military officer spoke out what he believed, what he had received as a revelation. He declared his hope and confidence. You and I can function like this. When God gives us a download regarding an area of our lives, or the lives of someone we care about, we too can move from hope to action. We too can step into the Faith Zone.

The Faith Zone is where miracles happen. The Faith Zone is where God steps in and big rewards follow.

Let me pray for you.

> *Father, thank you so much for stories like that of this centurion who had great faith. Thank you that we too can believe for more than we have right now. Father you want us to push for our breakthroughs and to become overcomers. Father, reveal your heart to us. When you do*

speak; help us to treasure what you say. Then help us to act. We pray
this in Jesus' name, Amen.

GOING DEEPER

1. Ask the Lord to speak to you about your destiny. "Lord, what are you planning for me in the next few years?"

2. Ask the Lord what your action steps need to be to get to that point?

3. One final journaling question: "What do I need to know today to prepare for my destiny?"

ENDNOTE

[1]Roger Sapp, allnationsmin.org

CHAPTER 4

The Little Faith of the Disciples
MATTHEW 8

Then he got into the boat and his disciples followed him. Suddenly a furious storm came up on the lake, so that the waves swept over the boat. But Jesus was sleeping. The disciples went and woke him, saying, "Lord, save us. We're going to drown." He replied, "You of little faith, why are you so afraid?" Then he got up and rebuked the winds and the waves, and it was completely calm. The men were amazed and asked, "What kind of man is this? Even the winds and the waves obey him." **MATTHEW 8:23-27**

Matthew, the former tax collector, wrote one of the biographies of Jesus. Being one of the Twelve gave him a front row seat. He saw the miracles, he heard the public talks, and he was with Jesus for the private discussions.

When Matthew wrote his narrative it is probable that Mark's biography was already in the public domain. Mark wrote a very succinct overview of Jesus, largely following the events chronologically. Matthew chose a unique path for his book. His target audience was Messianic Jews.

He wrote in themes. The healing stories of Jesus are largely grouped together, as are the parables and the teachings of Jesus.

Matthew 8 combines healing stories and faith stories. Matthew would not have had chapter divisions; he simply wrote topically. Along with the Roman centurion's faith statement, he recounts a leper's healing, the healing of Peter's mother-in-law, a crowd's healing, two demonized men's healings, and this story of the disciples' little faith.

The unique part of the story of little faith is that Matthew is describing something that personally happened to him. The story isn't a positive one, yet one he wants included in his biography. He may have been an active contributor of that little faith, perhaps even the one whom Jesus rebuked.

I believe that Matthew purposely places this story in with the healing accounts. I'm confident that Matthew wants his readers to understand the difference between great faith and little faith. I believe these divergent stories serve a purpose when placed together. Great faith, as we saw in the previous chapter, is characterized as acting on revelation with great confidence. Little faith is knowing something, but not moving forward with assurance. Let me prove my theory.

STORMS ON THE SEA OF GALILEE

First some background to set the scene. It would appear that four of Jesus' Twelve were experienced fishermen. It is probable that they worked in a consortium with Peter as their leader. Matthew 4:18–22 tells us of two sets of brothers, Peter and Andrew, plus James and John, the sons of Zebedee. All four were fishermen and part of the Twelve. In John 20:1-3 we read that Peter told six others that he was going fishing. The other six agreed, and headed out for a night of fishing. In this list we have five of the Twelve named: Peter, James and John, Thomas and Nathanael.

My point is this: at least four of the twelve disciples are experienced sailors on the Sea of Galilee. It is very possible that several others, such as Thomas and Nathanael, were also fishermen and would have known these waters.

The narrative begins with Jesus ordering them to set sail. *"When Jesus saw the crowd around him, he gave orders to cross to the other side of the lake"* (Matthew 8:18).

The word for *orders* is a strong one. Perhaps Jesus was fed up with the compromise of the people. A teacher and a disciple, not one of the Twelve, had both asked to be part of His inner circle. Because they had other priorities, Jesus dismissed them harshly (Matthew 8:19-21).

Jesus is the first to board the small boat and then the rest also get aboard. *"Then he got into the boat and his disciples followed him"* Matthew 8:22. Being the first in the boat, Jesus promptly finds a spot on the floor and falls asleep (Matthew 8:24). He takes up some valuable floor space.

THE JESUS BOAT

Let me tell you about this boat. If you are on a tour of Israel, one of the places to visit is the Jesus Boat Museum near Tiberius. Here you will find a first century boat that would have been very similar to the ones Jesus used. This particular boat was discovered in 1986, along the northwest shore of the Sea of Galilee. It took twelve days to excavate and seven years to preserve the wood so it could be exposed to air and not evaporate. Apparently this boat was well used. The museum estimates that it sailed on the lake for upwards of a hundred years.

According to one website, the boat is made of twelve different types of wood and measures 25.5 feet long (8.2 m), 7.5 feet wide (2.3 m), and is 4.1 feet high (1.25 m). It would have had a crew of five, four rowers and a helmsman, and could carry about fifteen additional people.[1]

So, we have a small fishing or transport boat headed from Capernaum at the north end of the lake to Genersert on the eastern side of the lake. The drive time is fifteen minutes. Sailing the 4 miles (7 km) would be dependent on the wind. Well this particular day was very windy. The NIV translation of the Bible uses the word *"furious storm"* to describe how bad the conditions were (Matthew 8:24).

The Sea of Galilee is small by Canadian Great Lakes standards. It is only 33 miles in circumference (55 km). It is shaped similar to a tooth with a length of 13 miles (21 km) and a width of 8 miles (13 km) on the north end. There are hills completely surrounding the lake. In the story of Jesus travel-ing from Tiberius north to where the feeding of the 5000+ took place, we read that people traveled on foot and were waiting for him when he arrived (Matthew 14:13–14). I often wonder how they would have known where his boat was heading and be able to get there before Jesus. The reason is the hills. If word got out that Jesus was heading north in a boat, the people would all have been able to see the boat on a clear day. From almost every perspective, you could see the whole of the lake.

At the northwest corner of the lake there is a small gap in the surrounding hills. Every tour guide I've had has told us that westerly winds come from the Mediterranean and blow through this natural funnel into the Sea of Galilee. If the winds are harsh, a storm ensues. Because of the hills around the lake, the wind is naturally contained within the circumference of the lake. It blows around and around stirring up the waves and making it very hard for sailors to get anywhere. Picture what happens to the water in a toilet bowl when you flush. That is what these Sea of Galilee storms are like.

On our tours to Israel one of the highlights is to take a tourist boat from Tiberius to the Jesus Boat Museum, which is very near where Jesus fed the five thousand. Every time we have been on this lake it has been calm with no wind. We feed bread to the seagulls. We worship Jesus in a very peaceful and tranquil environment. Looking at the open gap between the hills, we can imagine what it would be like to be in a small 25-foot boat in a furious storm. It would not be pretty. It would be terrifying. Sails would not help. Strong oarsmen would have great difficulty getting to shore and safety.

The Twelve, including Matthew, and including at least four experienced sailors, are in a life-threatening situation. "*The waves swept over the boat. But Jesus was sleeping. The disciples went and woke him, saying, 'Lord, save us. We're going to drown'*" (Matthew 8:24–25). I don't know how Jesus was able to sleep through a storm. Somehow, even when the waves were splashing over the sides, Jesus stayed sound asleep. I'm guessing that Jesus either had no stress in his life, or he was very tired. Probably both.

DEEP-SEA FISHING WITH JACK FROST

I know what it is like to be seasick. Not a good feeling. Years ago Jack and Tricia Frost hosted our pastors for a retreat in Myrtle Beach, South Carolina. Jack took some of us deep-sea fishing one morning. My experience can't be called deep-sea fishing. It was more like deep-sea throwing up. My recollection is that I got sick seventeen times in the eight hours we were on the boat. Everything was going well until the waves started picking up.

We were in a 40-foot ship with a large deck to fish from. There was a small cabin where we could watch the captain navigate and be out of the rain. Below the bridge were two bunk beds, a small toilet, and the engine room. We were told by the deckhand that if we felt we were going to be sick to do two things. First, don't look at the waves, but rather the horizon. The problem with that advice was the horizon kept moving. Waves blocked my view. Second, if we were thinking of throwing up, move to the side and get sick overboard. This wasn't to help our seasickness, but rather so he didn't have to clean up after us. I began to despise the deckhand.

Well I had the honour of being the first one to throw up. I had the honour to be the first one to throw up a second time. I was honoured all morning and into the afternoon. The only one of our pastoral team to not get sick was also the only gal onboard. Dawn Critchley, the wife of one of our worship pastors at the time, loved fishing and found the situation slightly humourous. Even John Arnott got sick a couple times.

I had bought some of those anti-seasickness pressure point things that you put on your wrists. John Arnott and the others thought it very funny that I was the only one to be wearing them and was the first to throw up. I began to despise them too. Seasickness can give you delusional thoughts. Radical ideas came to me as I stood along the railing feeding the fish with my vomit. The ideas all related to me jumping overboard. Somehow this seemed a more rational idea than throwing up on the boat. My mind told me that swimming back to the port, a mere 40 miles away, was better than being trapped on this boat.

Realizing that this wasn't a good idea, I forced myself away from the rail and found one of the lower bunks. Lying down actually was a good thing. I threw up far less while lying down. Perhaps this was why Jesus was sleeping in the bottom of the boat. Every so often I felt better. *Perhaps I should go up to the deck and try fishing*, I thought. I would climb the stairs to the deck, I'd see the waves and throw up again. I stayed in the bunk until we were a few miles from dry land.

I had three companions in the bunks. Jeremy Sinnott, another of our worship pastors, Ahren Summach, our youth pastor, and Fred Wright, who was leading Partners in Harvest at the time. All of us were sick. Fred didn't even bother to get up and head to the rail to throw up. He had found a ziplock bag and simply unzipped it whenever he felt the need. No one was laughing at me now, this was serious seasickness.

I remember the feeling that came to me when we headed for home. Seeing the first sight of land brought me greater joy than most other experiences I have had in life. I cheerfully helped with unloading the fish that were caught by the others. I took my unused fishing rod ashore. I smiled with great relief when my feet hit the dock. I had survived. Jack Frost, the captain of our chartered boat, the deckhand, and Dawn Critchley, were the only ones unscathed. The captain looked at us with mild disgust. I looked at him with disdain; he had taken us out in stormy weather. Plus, I paid $60 to do this.

Turns out we weren't in a storm, just a normal fishing day with 8-foot waves. I've seen the movie *The Perfect Storm*. I watch *Deadliest Catch* on television. No thanks. I'm not doing that again.

FEAR OF DROWNING

I can imagine that Matthew, a tax collector, would have been one of the first men to suggest that getting in the boat was not a good idea. Thomas would have been having a heyday, second guessing Peter and the other guys who manned the sails or rowed.

It is one thing for people like me to react in a storm, but it would appear that even the professional sailors onboard were terrified and frightened for their lives. We don't know who it is, but one of the Twelve woke Jesus up. Why did they wake Jesus up? Was Jesus an experienced sailor? No, he was a builder. Did Jesus have a history of being around the water? No, he lived in Nazareth until he was 30 years old. Nazareth isn't near any lakes. While boats are mentioned 50 times in the Gospels, there is no evidence to say that Jesus had any technical skills that Peter and the other guys lacked. Jesus didn't have naval engineering experience that warranted the guys seeking his advice on handling this boat.

So, why would experienced, professional sailors and fishermen turn to a passenger during this crisis? They woke Jesus up because they felt he could help them. Their revelation, which no doubt came from seeing numerous healings and miracles, was that Jesus somehow might be able to help them. I think the key phrase is *may be able*. They are desperate. They fear drowning. *"The disciples went and woke him, saying, 'Lord, save us. We're going to drown'"* (Matthew 8:25).

In every chapter of this book we are going to look at how faith works, through the stories of the Scriptures. What we've determined so far is that faith is acting on revelation.

So, what was the revelation that these mighty men of God had? They say it. *"Lord, save us. We're going to drown"* (Matthew 8:25). The disciples believed that Jesus can save them from drowning. This revelation was not based on his navigational skills. They were hoping that Jesus somehow, someway, would do something to keep them alive. They needed a miracle and Jesus knew how to do miracles.

Their faith action was waking Jesus up. This they did with expectancy and urgency.

WHAT IS LITTLE FAITH?

Have you ever woken up and been in a bit of a daze, unsure of where you are? It appears that Jesus had one of those moments. Look at the text: *"He replied, 'You of little faith, why are you so afraid?' Then he got up and rebuked the winds and the waves, and it was completely calm"* (Matthew 8:26).

Jesus asked why they were afraid. He said this before he gets up. He hasn't noticed the storm yet. Lying in the boat, Jesus would not have seen the waves because the sides of boat were blocking his view. He may have heard the wind. He may have felt the water slushing at his feet. He may have grasped that the ship was heaving in the waves, but he didn't panic. Before Jesus does anything about the wind and waves, before he stands or sits up; he makes a simple declaration, and then he asks a profound question.

You of little faith, why are you so afraid? MATTHEW 8:26

What Jesus was questioning is their revelation.
If they have revelation that Jesus can do something, why are they afraid? If they know in their heart of hearts that he can save them, why the urgency, why the drama?

Good observation, Jesus.
So let's speculate a bit.

If the Roman centurion had been with them, how would someone with greater faith have reacted? The military man understood that Jesus didn't need to be directly involved in his servant's healing. All he needed Jesus for was to say the word. If the soldier was in the boat he may have woken Jesus up and said something like "Jesus, sorry to bother you right now, but we have a problem. Can you take five seconds and tell the storm to shut up so we can all go back to sleep?"

Would you agree that this would have been greater faith?
What would even greater faith have looked like?

Great faith would have been one of the disciples, any of them, standing up and doing the miracle himself. One of them has the revelation. *I know we can get Jesus to do this, but since he is sleeping, let me say the words...* "Winds and waves, stop."

But that isn't what happened. The disciples do wake Jesus up and they do ask him to do something, anything. Their revelation was small. They have, in Jesus' words, *"little faith."*

FAITH IS FULL OF EXPECTATION

The parallel passage of this story comes from Luke, who wasn't on the boat. Luke would have had to interview one or more of the Twelve to find out what really happened. Luke's account contains one little fact that Matthew forgot, or chose not to include.

We see it in Luke 8:22: *"One day Jesus said to his disciples, 'Let us go over to the other side of the lake.' So they got into a boat and set out."* Before they get in the boat on the north shores of the Sea of Galilee, Jesus had made a simple, yet profound statement. *"Let us go over to the other side of the lake."*

What was Jesus' expectation for this short 5-mile voyage? Jesus expected they would get to the other side. They would get there alive. If all of the disciples heard Jesus say this, why are they worried and fearful? Didn't Jesus promise them a safe arrival? Jesus said nothing about the journey itself, but he did say they would get to the other side. *"Let us..."*

So instead of confidence in what Jesus said about the final outcome, the men were focused on the middle part of the journey. They were concerned about the now. Their confidence in getting to the other side was challenged by the looming threat of drowning. What they see in the storm outweighed what they heard Jesus say.

Fears and faith work side by side almost all of the time. Do the disciples hold on to Jesus' words or do they believe the evidence provided by their eyes and ears? The devil's words would have been bombarding them with thoughts like "be worried, be very worried." If faith is acting on a revelation from God, then fear is acting on a revelation from Satan. Fear is as simple as listening to the wrong voice. The last chapter of this book will focus on this battle in greater detail.

If one of the Twelve, any of them, had said to the panicked group, "Hold it guys, before Jesus fell asleep he told us to wake him up when we got to shore. Remember his words? He said we'd get to the other side." Is it possible that one disciple would have changed the narrative? But none of them had confidence in what they heard Jesus say. No one valued his words. So instead of a confident assurance, which is a part of the faith process, anxiety resulted in fear.

The Twelve did have some faith, some revelation, but not the kind in the *great* category. Rather, Jesus categorized it as "*little.*" They could have taken care of the winds and waves themselves. That would have been great faith. They should have let their leader sleep and be refreshed. But their confidence was in Jesus' action, not in their own.

Then he (Jesus) got up and rebuked the winds and the waves, and it was completely calm. MATTHEW 8:26

After a quick comment (*little faith*) and a question (*why are you afraid*), Jesus gets up from the floor. He stands, probably holding both railings, and simply rebukes the wind and waves. Matthew's simple summary is that *"it was completely calm."* The inference is that the change was instantaneous. The storm ceased in a second. Amazing.

The reaction of frightened people is often comical. My grandsons will either cry, laugh, or look at me with bewilderment. "Why would you scare me?" Matthew and Luke both record the same reaction. The men are shocked and have no grid for what just happened.

The men were amazed and asked, "What kind of man is this? Even the winds and the waves obey him." MATTHEW 8:27

Their reaction tells us something more about the level of revelation they had regarding Jesus at this moment. Remember when we talked about them having confidence that Jesus could do something? Well, this something wasn't in their grid. What happened to the wind and waves was way past their revelation. I have no idea what they were expecting, but it wasn't a calm sea.

Perhaps their revelation was that Jesus, having just slept, would be strong enough to hold the sails or take over rowing to the closest point of land. Perhaps they felt that Jesus would be able to slightly calm down the wind or the waves, but not to this extent. They are absolutely overwhelmed by what Jesus did.

Let's go back to the Roman centurion. What was his expectation when he told Jesus that he didn't need him at the house but to *"just say the word"* (Matthew 8:8)? He expected a healing. What did he get? He got a great healing. His great faith produced a great healing. His servant was instantly healed without Jesus being at the home. There was no prayer, no touch, just one word: *"Go."*

We have talked about rewards. Did you know that even little faith gets rewarded? Because the disciples had a little faith, they got a little miracle. If instantly bringing peace to the wind and waves comes with little faith, I have no clue what a great miracle would have been. Perhaps they would have teleported instantly to the shore on the other side of the lake, to a nice coffee shop. Perhaps they would have levitated and walked on clouds to their next appointment. Perhaps a giant fish would have appeared, swallowed them and spit them out on the shore. I have no clue, but when we get to heaven we can ask Jesus what great faith would have looked like for that storm.

My point is that God had better plans up his sleeve, if only one of the Twelve had had more than a little faith. There was a better reward waiting for them. In later chapters we are going to see a phrase that is full of hope, as well as full of caution. The phrase is *"according to your faith, be it done to you."* (Matthew 9:29)

To the level that we act on our revelation of who God is and what Jesus can do for us, is the level the Holy Spirit can act in our lives. That is what determines what happens to us.

If we have no confidence in our revelations, then we will get what we have faith for: nothing. However, if we have a high level of confidence in our revelation of who God is and what he can do, then we will get great rewards.

Do you remember Hebrews 11:6? *"And without faith it is impossible to please God, because anyone who comes to him must believe that he exists and that he rewards those who earnestly seek him."* If you and I don't act in faith, we do not please God. We disqualify ourselves from the rewards that the Lord has waiting for us. The Twelve had a little reward when in actuality God had a greater reward ready for them. They did have a little bit of faith. They did believe that Jesus could do something. But it could have been so much better.

WHAT ABOUT US?

The principle of this story is simple; knowing that Jesus can help us when we are in trouble is a beginner's revelation. Three-year-olds have this basic understanding.

God wants us to have a far greater revelation of what He can do for us. God wants us to believe his words and act on them.

Words like...

"With God all things are possible." **MATTHEW 19:16**

"I am with you always, to the very end of the age." **MATTHEW 28:20**

"Take courage. It is I. Don't be afraid." **MATTHEW 14:27**

So the question for each one of us as we conclude this chapter is this:

What do we believe about Jesus?
What hope has God put into our spirit?
What revelations are in us that we can hold onto when life's stuff comes our way?

God bless Matthew for sharing a story that doesn't show him and the other disciples in a good light. Matthew included this story so we can understand the limitations that he and his buddies had at that stage of their journey. He doesn't want us to have the same limited view that he and his friends did of God's abilities.

Stories like this one give me great confidence. Will I always get it right? No. Will I always act with great faith? Probably not. But I can start where I am. I can act on small revelations, on simple things. I can begin to digest the Scriptures and hold His promises as true. I can act with simplicity and see God reward me.

I can also learn to take bolder actions with the greater revelations I have. I can act on revelation and when I do, God will reward me.

> *Father, thank you for inspiring Matthew to share this story with us. Thank you that he reveals a time when he and the disciples didn't act with confidence, but rather showed little faith. Father would you help us when the storms of life come. Help us not to panic or to forget your promises. Help us to know that you are always taking us to the other side. Father, please help us grow in our faith. Help us to mature from little faith to great faith. In Jesus' name we pray. Amen.*

GOING DEEPER

1. Ask the Lord to remind you of a time when you were fearful. Where were you? Ask Jesus to reveal to you what Satan's lie was. Ask Jesus to reveal himself to you in that situation. When you see or sense Jesus with you, tell him what Satan said. Then ask Jesus what the truth is. Write down what Jesus says.

2. Once you hear the truth you have a choice. Accept what Satan said or accept what Jesus said. What is your choice? If you choose Jesus, welcome his truth to bring more freedom. Repent for believing Satan's lie, renounce it, and command the lie to be gone from your heart and mind.

3. You may need to forgive some people associated with this time in your past. Do that. Picture them and the situation and say, "I forgive and release and honor you in Jesus' name." You may need to repent of making vows (statements such as "I'll never..." or "I'll always..."). Do that. You may need to renounce judgements against people or organizations. Do that.

ENDNOTE

[1] Sacred Destinations, *Jesus Boat Museum, Tiberias* (retrieved December 2015) http://www.sacred-destinations.com/israel/jesus-boat

CHAPTER 5

The Faith of Four Friends

MATTHEW 9

Jesus stepped into a boat, crossed over and came to his own town. Some men brought to him a paralyzed man, lying on a mat. When Jesus saw their faith, he said to the man, "Take heart, son; your sins are forgiven." At this, some of the teachers of the law said to themselves, "This fellow is blaspheming." Knowing their thoughts, Jesus said, "Why do you entertain evil thoughts in your hearts? Which is easier: to say, 'Your sins are forgiven,' or to say, 'Get up and walk'? But I want you to know that the Son of Man has authority on earth to forgive sins." So he said to the paralyzed man, "Get up, take your mat and go home." Then the man got up and went home. When the crowd saw this, they were filled with awe; and they praised God, who had given such authority to man. **MATTHEW 9:1–8**

One of the purposes of this book is to show that the faith process isn't supposed to be hard. Most of the faith stories that we are looking at are ones where a person exhibited confidence in what they heard God say. They acted on the revelation they received from the Lord and saw a breakthrough. That is how we enter the Faith Zone.

The phrase *"according to your faith"* is both a positive and negative (Matthew 9:29). If God rewards based on our actions, then I have a part to play. I can activate what I need. I can also stall and postpone what God would like to happen by my inactivity. A pitfall for some of us is living in a place where we don't expect God to speak to us. We aren't sure that if God spoke we'd be able to recognize his voice. If we don't ever receive God's thoughts, how are we to act in faith?

THE PRAYER OF FAITH

Here is some good news: I actually don't have to have my own faith to see a breakthrough. I can act according to the faith of others.

James, the leader of the first church in Jerusalem, had confidence in the elders of his ministry. He knew that when people were sick, the prayers of his leaders would heal them.

> The prayer offered in faith will make the sick person well; the Lord will raise
> them up, if they have sinned they will be forgiven. JAMES 5:15

James expects his leaders to pray in faith. This is great news. The faith of spiritual leaders can help me, even if I don't have the same level of hope. If a ministry team member, if a pastor, if a small group leader, has revelation about my needs, their faith can usher in my breakthrough. Jesus' healing prayers weren't the type of prayers we can say full of doubt and unbelief. They were commands. James is saying that the simple, to-the-point prayers of a person who knows God's heart gets results.

The prayer of faith isn't a maybe, could you, will you, if-it-is-your-will type of prayer. It is "Be clean" (Matthew 8:3), "Go" (Matthew 8:13), "Get up, take your mat and go home" (Matthew 9:6). It is a command prayer with full authority and power from heaven.

Perhaps the best story to illustrate that we can benefit from the faith of others is found in the passage we read at the beginning of this chapter from Matthew 9. A man needs a miracle. He is paralyzed, unable to walk, and restricted to a begging mat (Matthew 9:2). We don't know much about him other than his restrictions and that he lives in Capernaum (Mark 2:1).

On the upside, great miracles have already taken place in this town. We looked at some of them in chapter three when we talked about the Roman centurion. This lame man lived in a community with high expectations for the miraculous to take place whenever Jesus was in town.

We do know that the man has four friends that care about him (Mark 2:3). We have no ages, no names, no job titles. We do know that they had hope for their disabled friend and were willing to act on it. This story of these friends made such an impression on the Twelve that it is included in three of the Gospel accounts: Matthew's (chapter 9:1–8); Mark's (chapter 2:1–12); and Luke's (chapter 5:17–26). Luke's version fills in more details regarding their faith journey. We find out that Jesus had a planned meeting in Capernaum. Pharisees and teachers of the law have gathered from the two regions of Israel: Galilee in the north and Judea in the south. Some have even come from as far as Jerusalem to be at this event (Luke 5:17).

FAITH STARTS WITH A GOD-THOUGHT

When news broke that Jesus was in town, at least one of the four buddies had a God-thought. The thought was probably as simple as "let's take our paralyzed friend to the meeting—Jesus can heal him if we get him there."

> *Some men came carrying a paralyzed man on a mat and tried to take him into the house to lay him before Jesus.* LUKE 5:18

Obstacles and revelation almost always pair up; something usually comes up that makes the faith process hard. Whether it is Satan against us or our Father strengthening us and wanting us to push through, stuff happens to challenge our God-thoughts. We will spend a whole chapter talking about obstacles later.

When the four men arrived, there was a big problem—others had also heard that Jesus was in town and a large crowd had formed.

> *A few days later, when Jesus again entered Capernaum, the people heard that he had come home. They gathered in such large numbers that there was no room left, not even outside the door, and he preached the word to them.* MARK 2:1-2

Problem. The venue where Jesus was meeting with the religious leaders was already full. Not only was the house full, but the four friends couldn't even get close to the house because of the crowd. *There was no room left, not even outside the door.* (Mark 2:2) For those of you who have been in Capernaum you will know how narrow the streets are; there is barely room for two people to walk together. It is possible that this home was either near the market or near the synagogue, where space was more open.

Remember I said that faith is supposed to be easy? Let me show you how the process of moving from hope to faith works in this story. You'll see that if we persist, we can get the breakthroughs we need for ourselves, or our friends and family.

These four men have a God-thought: "Let's take our friend to Jesus so he can heal him." They act on the revelation that they are given. They take him to where Jesus is meeting. This is good. But there is a crowd. This is a problem. They now have a choice. They can second guess their original thought and take their disabled friend home. They could have justified doing this. "Hey we tried." "We simply got there too late." "There were others ahead of us." "Better luck next time." All of these types of thoughts come from Satan. They are doubt revelations.

GOD LOVES TO GIVE SECOND CHANCES

Because God loves us and because he doesn't want us to miss any of his destiny purposes, he gave these four men another revelation. God loves helping us to live in faith. He made it easy for them to push forward.

"If we can't get our friend through the crowd, or through the front door, let's drop him in through the roof!"

When they could not find a way to do this because of the crowd, they went up
on the roof and lowered him on his mat through the tiles into the middle of the
crowd, right in front of Jesus. LUKE 5:19

They take their friend through the back streets to the other side of the home. Up they go to the roof. They begin to remove the mud and dirt that serves as insulation. Then up come the tiles so they can lower their friend through the hole. "This idea will definitely get the attention of Jesus—he will have to do something, right?"

Houses in Capernaum, as in most of Israel, had flat roofs. The homes were small, with only a couple of rooms. People didn't live in their homes; they lived outside. The toilet wasn't in the house, but behind a tree. Food was cooked over an open flame outside, not a fancy stovetop and oven. Large living areas or bedrooms did not exist. A family would share one or two rooms. You sat outside with other families. The only time you stayed inside was during inclement weather. Houses were built from rocks and mud. At the Capernaum excavations you can see the ancient stones that framed the homes in this town. The rock walls of the homes are about 18 inches (45 cm) wide. No high ceilings in those days, just functional, low maintenance homes.

Whether there was a ladder nearby or some sort of stairs to get to the roof, we don't know. We don't know how thick the roof is. What we do know is that once up there, they begin to dig out the rocks and dirt to get down to the base tiles. Luke's version of the story tells us that the roof had tiles. "*They made an opening in the roof above Jesus by digging through it*" (Mark 2:4). Mark's narrative adds that there was a layer of something, probably mud and dirt, that they first had to dig through to get to the tiles. *"They lowered him, on his mat through the tiles into the middle of the crowd"* (Luke 5:19).

INSIDE THE HOUSE

Imagine what it was like to be in this house. You're a religious leader who had a special invite to meet with Jesus for a private consultation. More people came than the home could accommodate. Crowds are outside trying to get the attention of Jesus. The meeting begins. My guess is that while this crowd was opposed to Jesus, they came to hear him out. As the meeting progresses, one of the Scribes gets hit with a clump of dirt. Then another. And another.

The men look up, as does Jesus. The meeting stops as everyone watches what is happening above them. If the owner of the home is inside, I can imagine that he is yelling at them to stop. Perhaps he tries to get outside and onto the roof to force them to stop. Perhaps Jesus motions for him and the others to just be quiet and watch.

Spoiler alert: in a later chapter I will give you my comments as to who owns this home.

Eventually there is a large enough gap in the roof for the people below to see what this disturbance is all about. They see four men. The crowd watches as the men clear away a gap and begin to lower a mat with someone lying on it.

Since they could not get him to Jesus because of the crowd, they made an opening in the roof above Jesus by digging through it and then lowered the mat the man was lying on. MARK 2:4

FAITH CAN BE SEEN

All three of the gospel accounts tell us the same thing. While everyone saw the man being lowered by the four friends, Jesus sees something different. He sees their faith. *"When Jesus saw their faith, he said to the man, 'Take heart, son; your sins are forgiven.'"* (Matthew 9:2)

The key words are *"their faith."* We have two distinct possibilities as to what Jesus is talking about. The word "their" can refer to the four men, but it can also refer to the four men and the paralyzed man who is lying on the mat. We don't know. I'm going to assume that the primary reference is to the four friends. If that is correct, then their faith allowed for this miracle to take place. The handicapped man may not even have been a willing participant.

REVIEW HOW FAITH WORKS

Faith starts with a God-thought, then an action step, and then a reward. Going through this process takes us into the Faith Zone. The men hear that Jesus is in town. One of them says to the others, "Let's get our buddy to Jesus so he can be healed." They all agree with the revelation and react by taking him to the home.

Problem. There is a large obstacle that challenges their confidence. The other townsfolk got there ahead of the four friends. It's a sold-out venue. Also, a large crowd is waiting for the meeting to finish so they can connect with Jesus.

Solution. One of the men gets another thought: "Let's force the issue by lowering our friend through the roof." Agreed. They act again and after a few minutes of dirty work they lower the paralyzed man right in front of Jesus. Jesus discerns what has happened. He understands how revelation works. I can imagine a wry smile on his face as these guys anxiously lower the disabled man. Jesus gets it. They were acting on a revelation.

Their faith activates Jesus. Jesus steps out of teacher mode and into his healing anointing. Luke, a medical doctor, has added something in the prelude to his story that the others didn't include: *"and the power of the Lord was with Jesus to heal the sick"* (Luke 5:17).

I've written a book called *My Healing Belongs to Me.*[1] One of the chapters deals with this very sentence. To summarize simply, wherever Jesus was, healing was possible. It just needed to be activated. Because the Spirit of the Lord was on Jesus, anointing was always available for miracles (Acts 10:38). All Jesus needed to kick-start the anointing was for someone to have faith. Anyone.

The man's need for healing clearly motivated the four friends to get him to Jesus. Twice they acted on the God-thoughts they were given. They overcame an obstacle that would have stopped most of us. The key is they didn't stop listening and acting. Faith is being confident of what we know. These men did not give up on the original idea that they had—get the paralyzed friend to Jesus and Jesus will do something to help him.

Now, as they lower their buddy into the room, Jesus smiles and nods his head. He begins to act. Jesus now begins to listen to what his Father was telling him to do. His Spirit knows that they are acting in faith. This inspires Jesus to act accordingly.

A quick thought comes to Jesus about how his Father wants to minister to this man. The Father whispers to Jesus that the core issue for this one is forgiveness. With that knowledge, Jesus begins to minister. *"When Jesus saw their faith, he said to the man, 'Take heart, son; your sins are forgiven'"* (Matthew 9:2).

HEALING IN THE HOUSE

While this next part isn't the primary focus of this chapter, let me say a few points on the actual healing. Jesus' first response is to deal with the root problem that is blocking the man's restoration. Jesus didn't go straight to healing. There is a sin issue, something to do with the man needing to be forgiven. God would have given Jesus enough revelation to know how to act.

Jesus forgives the man who is now lying in front of him and still lame. Forgiveness is a powerful, powerful tool that we somehow still haven't fully grasped. We don't know if the man has asked for forgiveness as he was being lowered or if Jesus has simply sensed his heart condition. The crowd, religious men, takes offence that Jesus is talking this way. They are not aware that mere people are able to forgive sins. They think only God can do this. *"At this, some of the teachers of the law said to themselves, 'This fellow is blaspheming'"* (Matthew 9:3).

Jesus asks them a very interesting question: "*Which is easier: to say, 'Your sins are forgiven,' or to say, 'Get up and walk?'*" (Matthew 9:5). Apparently, healing is easier. Jesus, seeing the stubbornness in their hearts, decides to do both. To prove that he can forgive sins, he says a command. Not a prayer—a command. "*So he said to the paralyzed man, 'Get up, take your mat and go home'*" (Matthew 9:6).

What happens next is miraculous. "*Then the man got up and went home*" (Matthew 9:7). Jesus commands him to get up, and he does. In His pronouncement of forgiveness, Jesus deals with the root issue. With the core issue out of the way, the next part of the healing was easy. He commanded him to walk.

By the way, for those of you who wonder if inner healing has relevance today, this passage says yes. Jesus dealt with many root issues in his healing ministry. He dealt with physical diseases and pain, demonic strongholds, unforgiveness, sin, etc. Any of these in our lives gives Satan access to bring sickness and steal our health.

THE CROWD'S REACTION

The crowd in the home had no option but to switch from disapproval to praise and worship. "*When the crowd saw this, they were filled with awe; and they praised God, who had given such authority to man*" (Matthew 9:8). The crowd would be referring to those who were inside the home as well as those outside. They would have seen the four men on the roof. They would have seen them lifting their paralyzed friend up to the roof. They would also have seen the lame man lowered into the room.

You can imagine that those by the windows and doors of the home would be yelling to those behind them, giving them a play-by-play.

"He's standing!"

Shock ripples sweep through the crowd.
"What?" "Are you sure?" "What happened?"
"I don't know, but he's bending over and rolling up his stretcher mat."

And then the man, who used to be paralyzed, walks out the door, through the crowd, to his home. Amazing! I love how this faith thing works.

WHO ACTIVATED THE MIRACLE?

Let's back up and take one more look at this remarkable story. What was it that enabled Jesus to heal the man? It was the faith of the four friends. This miracle didn't start with Jesus. It started with one (or more) friend acting on a God-thought.

Someone reads in the morning paper that Jesus is in town. He reads the address of that night's meeting. The man calls three others and they head to the home of the lame man. With or without his approval, the friends take him to the meeting to act on what they believe to be a God-inspired revelation.

As they approach the home their hope begins to wane. "Look at all the people." "How are we ever going to get him in?" Perhaps one of them leaves the others and tries to get closer. "Can't be done."

When it seems like their hope is lost, another thought comes to one of the men. "Let's rip up the roof tiles and get him in that way—Jesus will have to do something then."

They had faith that Jesus would respond to their actions and the events unfolded according to their faith. Jesus did act and their friend was miraculously healed. The paralyzed man who needed a miracle benefited from the faith of his friends. Their faith brought his breakthrough. They were able to take him into the Faith Zone.

You too can access a great miracle for your friends. In turn they can help you with your breakthroughs. I hope your mind is racing right now with God-thoughts—thoughts of what God can do about your own needs, and those of your friends. Write them down, or get out your smart phone and record them. These thoughts are from Father God.

MY FIRST HEALING OF A CRIPPLE

I tell this story in *My Healing Belongs to Me*, but it fits here as well. So if you have read that book, please forgive the repetition. If you haven't read it, this story is one of the first miracles I saw and participated in at Catch The Fire Toronto.

For many years I led a Sunday night healing meeting. We would have hundreds of people from Toronto and the surrounding region come to this focused meeting. One particular meeting, we had a guest speaker named Clive Pick. He was going to talk about finances. Because we had a focus on financial breakthroughs that weekend, a slightly different crowd came. One of them was a man named Carl who lived in Detroit.

Carl, as we later found out, had a lot of health problems. The cartilage in his knees had deteriorated over the last seventeen years. He relied on a cane, then a walker, and ultimately a wheelchair. Carl had a full-time nurse who was with him at the meeting. Carl also had diabetes, bladder problems, and, most notably, he was a haemophiliac. Derek Bishop and I were leading the meeting that particular Sunday evening. Derek was a retired pastor and one of our cell leaders.

That afternoon, while I was having my Sunday nap, I had a dream. In the dream the Lord told me that healing was going to be very easy that night. He also said that I was to do "show and tell, and not be religious." I knew what show and tell meant. It is where I demonstrate healing and then talk about it, rather than talk about it and then do it. I knew what religious meant. I wasn't to pray or to invoke the name of Jesus. I was to simply pronounce someone healed like Jesus did.

When I got to the meeting I told Derek what I felt we were supposed to do. He agreed but wanted me to go first. So, after the band finished leading our worship set, I asked everyone who needed a healing to come to the front. More than 50 people stood on our green ministry lines. I picked a woman to come on the stage for show and tell. I asked her what her problem was. She responded by saying she had pain in her wrists due to typing at her work. She called the problem carpal tunnel. I knew how this ailment worked because I've experienced it. Even the slightest wrist movements can cause pain.

I asked her where she lived. She said Welland, which was a two-hour drive away. I then went on a bit of a rabbit trail by asking her if she remembered a particular grocery store in Welland. She did. I told her that I used to service a vending machine in that store and described to everyone how it worked. It was a kid's game with a ceramic chicken that would cluck and lay an egg, which had a toy inside. She remembered this and we all laughed.

Just then I heard the Lord's internal signal that I had been waiting for. A "ding," like a microwave going off. This sound is one of the ways I know to stop ministering and tell folks that they are healed. So I wrapped up the chicken machine conversation and declared that she had been healed. She looked at me slightly confused because I hadn't prayed for her, I hadn't talked about Jesus, nothing.

I didn't need to. I was acting on revelation. The Lord had told me to do show and tell and not to be religious. I did my part and then the Lord told me that he had done his part. I was expecting a healing. I was in a wonderful Faith Zone. She checked her wrists and said all the pain was gone, much to her shock as well as the crowd's. Bingo. I looked good and felt very confident. I was in the zone.

Derek was a bit surprised as well. He followed a more traditional route with the lady he ministered to. She shared her problem and Derek prayed for her. He commanded the pain to go in Jesus' name. It did and she too was healed.

Okay, now to part two: the folks standing on the lines. The Lord had said to me in the dream that this next part would be easy. Knowing that one of the secrets of increased anointing is to have agreement, I asked our prayer ministry team to pair up with each person at the front. Normally we keep the genders together during this kind of ministry.

Ed Koeker is a faithful, godly man at Catch The Fire. Ed has been on our prayer team for most of the last twenty years. He assisted me most of those Sunday nights. He also loves to laugh. He sees the humour in most aspects of life, except one. Ed has a wife with a physical impairment. Flo is in a wheelchair and suffers from bone problems. Perhaps because of his wife's condition, Ed paired up with Carl, who had wheeled himself to the front. I had the prayer team quickly interview each person to find out his or her need. I instructed them to place a hand at the source of the pain. Apparently Carl asked for prayer for his arms.

My prayer was very simple: *Jesus, what you did for these two ladies on the stage do for the rest of them.* We waited a few seconds and then I asked the people to check themselves and see what had changed.

I remember saying this confidently because of what the Lord had spoken to me during the afternoon nap. I asked for responses. Carl was one of the first to raise his hand to signal that something had happened. I went down from the stage with a handheld microphone and began to interview him. Carl had white towels wrapped around both arms. He told me that he was a haemophiliac. Because he couldn't walk and because he had no cartilage in his knees, he often fell. When he fell, he would bruise himself. He would bleed easily and therefore he had the towels wrapped around his arms to absorb the blood, as well as to hide the bruises.

He agreed to let us unwrap the towels. His arms were purple, full of open sores and large bruises. Then, something amazing and miraculous happened. The open sores on Carl's arms instantly scabbed. The bleeding stopped and his arms began to recover right in front of us. Wow. Apparently we were still in the Faith Zone where the miraculous happens. Carl then dropped a small bomb. He told me that while Ed had prayed for him, he had been able to stand. I found out that he had suffered for seventeen years from severe knee problems. He told me that he had had surgery after surgery to repair both knees and nothing had worked.

His knees had no cartilage. Nothing was holding the lower legs to his femurs other than the skin around the knees. For him to say that he had been standing after Ed's prayer was shocking.

Ed didn't know all of Carl's problems before he prayed for him. Ed was simply following the directions that Derek and I gave for the ministry time. When I heard Carl say that he had stood, I remembered what the Lord had spoken to me that afternoon. Healing was going to be easy. Faith Zone, here we come. I asked Carl if he could try to stand again. He agreed. Ed and another man helped him to his feet. I remember him being wobbly. The two men supported Carl, helping to balance him.

I then had a God-thought. Why not go for it? So far everything the Lord had said to me in my dream was happening as he said it would. I was in the flow of listening, doing, and seeing breakthroughs. I asked Carl if he would like to try to walk a few steps. He agreed. I don't even remember if we prayed again or not.

Ed and the other man took Carl's arms and put them around their necks, like in a sporting match where the trainers carry an athlete hobbling to the sidelines. With most of his weight resting on these two men, Carl walked to where his wheelchair was, about 12 feet (4 meters) away.

What happened next was also not planned. Carl, standing by his wheelchair, did something none of us expected. He took his arms off the two men and stood unassisted. He proceeded to walk down the aisle of our auditorium. What?!

People began to applaud. Carl walked across the back of our auditorium. He walked down the other main aisle to where Derek was waiting for him. Everyone was in awe. This was an outstanding miracle.

Derek asked Carl how he was feeling. "Great," answered the man in his late seventies, adding, "I feel so good I think I can dance!"

I called the band up onto the stage. Owen Hurter, our worship leader that night, got the band to play an Irish jig. Derek and Carl walked up the stairs to the stage (about five steps without a handrail) and they both did a little dance. It was amazing! We have it all on video, as almost all of our meetings are recorded.

We found out the next day that all of Carl's other illnesses were also healed in that moment.

His diabetes was gone.
His arthritis was gone.
His bladder problem was gone.

His haemophiliac condition was gone.

The cartilage in his knees had returned.

He came to our church building the next day, walked onto the stage again and was a part of a television show that John and Carol Arnott were recording.

FAITH IS EASY

Easy. That was what the Lord had said to me. Faith Zone material. Good enough to include in a book on faith.

And it was easy. All I did was listen and act on the revelations as they came to me.

What Ed did was easy. He responded to the needs in Carl's life and said a simple healing prayer. What Carl did was easy. He responded to Ed's prayer with confidence. He stood when Ed asked him to. He took off his towels when I asked him to. He stood again when I asked him to. He took an assisted walk when I asked him to. Knowing that God was with him, Carl did what the Lord spoke into his heart the moment he reached his wheelchair. He literally stepped out in faith.

Two nights later, I had Carl share his story at my men's group. He told us that the Lord whispered a thought to him, something like "let go, and go for a walk." After hearing this, Carl let go of Ed and the other man. He stood for a second or two and then stepped forward. He acted on the God thought that he had just received. It meant taking a step, and he did just that. Easy. Carl was in the Faith Zone.

Friends, the revelation that I had while taking a nap contributed to Carl's healing. My part was a very small part. Derek's part was a small part. Carl's part was a small part. But together, our revelation-led actions resulted in a dramatic healing.

As you read this, have you been getting thoughts regarding a breakthrough that you need? Whatever the Lord spoke to you, I want you to begin to act. If you need to put this book down right now and make a phone call, do it. If you need to send an email, do it. Respond to your God-thoughts right now. Turn those hopes into faith. Have confidence that God can use you to usher in someone else's breakthrough.

If you are the one needing a miracle, begin to ask your friends to pray for you. Ask God to give them insights that you may have missed. Pray that God would speak to them, and that they would be brave enough to tell you what Father God said to do.

> When Jesus saw their faith, he said to the man, "Take heart, son; your sins are forgiven." MATTHEW 9:2

Let me pray for you.

> Father, I want to thank you for including this amazing story in three of the gospel accounts. Thank you that Matthew, Mark, and Luke all caught on to the point that the four friends were the keys to the

paralyzed man's healing. Father, you have friends like this for me. You have people who hear your voice when you speak. Others can help me receive my breakthrough. Father, bless my friends to hear you and to act on what they know is from you. Father, help me to be a friend to others as well. Help me to hear, to believe, and to act on the revelations that you give me for others. I want to thank you in advance that you want to make faith easy for me. Amen.

GOING DEEPER

1. Ask the Lord to bring to your mind someone you know well who needs a breakthrough. Ask the Lord to allow you to be the friend who has faith. Ask the Lord to speak to you about how you can take that person on a faith journey. Once the Lord speaks to you, act on it, do it.

2. Let's focus on a physical need you may have. I'd like you to picture yourself as the man on the mat being lowered before Jesus. Jesus sees you with eyes of compassion. What is it that Jesus needs to forgive you for? What is the first thought that comes to you? Repent for what you did, said, or thought. Renounce any vows, judgements, unforgiveness, etc. Now receive the word from Jesus to stand up and walk in wholeness.

ENDNOTE

[1]Steve Long, *My Healing Belongs to Me* (Catch The Fire Books, 2014).

CHAPTER 6

The Faith of the Haemorrhaging Woman

MATTHEW 9

As a child I liked to read books about pirates. It seemed to me that pirates had a wonderful life. Adventure after adventure. Treasure after treasure. I imagined finding a map and following the clues to find the treasure.

Treasure hunts are fun. As children of God, we can embark on a spiritual treasure hunt by listening to the Lord specifically to get revelation about a stranger. We can do this alone or in a group. The Lord will reveal details such as the colour of someone's clothes, age, walking a dog, etc. When you know what you are looking for, it makes it easy. There is just something about having a revelation on someone, writing it down, and then finding this stranger in person. It is very exhilarating.

Most Thursday nights our School of Ministry students head out to find treasures. The students go in pairs or groups of three. They spend some time worshiping in God's presence. They ask the Lord to show them someone he would like them to meet and minister to. On one particular night, two of our students were in a shopping mall near our church building.

They had a very detailed description of a woman that they had received from God. The team knew they were looking for a lady. They knew the colour of her clothes, her shoes, etc. They set out to find her.

When they spotted someone with a matching description, they simply went up to her and asked if she was their treasure. This always gets an inquisitive look. They explained what they were doing and showed the lady their clues. She was a young woman from Mexico. She was new to Canada, here without her family. She was lonely.

The School of Ministry students were so accurate in their description of her that she burst out crying. Turns out she had been praying to God to be able to meet people. She also had pain in her body. The team members prayed for her, and, as only God can do, she was healed right there on the spot. Because of their confidence, these two students had taken out their smart phones and taken a video as they walked through the mall looking for their treasure. I showed the footage to our church. These students were in the Faith Zone.

When God gave me the topic of faith for this book, I asked for insights. I wanted to write something that would be effective, helpful, and very practical. He told me to look in Matthew's gospel for stories of people who acted on a revelation. The acting on revelation that the Father gave me was a great treasure map. As I looked at the stories of Jesus in Matthew's account, I saw this theme of faith everywhere.

In fact, in most gospel stories where the word *faith* is used, we are usually told what the person's revelation was. We see their revelation, their action steps, and their rewards. It's all there in our Bible. God is trying to help each of us live by faith from the example of ancients. This pattern is true in this famous story of the woman from Capernaum who had the issue of bleeding.

PROBLEMS, REVELATIONS, ACTIONS AND REWARDS—THE FAITH PROCESS

Matthew shortens his narrative to three simple verses. In them we see her problem, her revelation, her action, and her reward. Perfect sermon points!

> Just then a woman who had been subject to bleeding for twelve years came up behind him and touched the edge of his cloak. She said to herself, "If I only touch his cloak, I will be healed." Jesus turned and saw her. "Take heart, daughter," he said, "your faith has healed you." And the woman was healed at that moment. MATTHEW 9:20-22

A UNIQUE PHYSICAL PROBLEM

What was her problem? She had a big one. Her menstrual period had been flowing non-stop for twelve years. Mark's gospel describes her challenge more fully: "She had suffered a great deal under the care of many doctors and had spent all she had; yet instead of getting better she grew worse" (Mark 5:26).

Mark tells us the doctors where not able to help her. Not only that, but she suffered a great deal under their care, or lack of it. I have no idea what kind of treatments doctors would give to help a woman stop bleeding.

I am sure that this was an extremely embarrassing procedure whatever it was. There was a huge medical breakthrough in the Middle ages regarding blood problems. It was called leeches. The idea was that bloodsuckers would drain the poison from your body. The medical technology in Jesus' day for blood issues wouldn't have been good. Whatever it was, leeches were an improvement.

It would appear that these medical procedures were also expensive. She spent all of her money, and still she wasn't any better. This had to be very discouraging. She was still bleeding and now poor. You can imagine the physical issues involved here. Fatigue from blood loss. Low blood pressure would lead to dizziness and imbalance. Her skin tone would change, and she would be short of breath much of the time.

RELIGIOUS PROBLEMS

On top of all her physical problems, there were the religious restrictions. Moses, in the book of Leviticus, outlined specific protocols for women on their menstrual cycle. Leviticus 15 records the instructions about emissions and blood. Both men and women would be unclean for a day if they had bodily secretions. Anyone they touched would be unclean for a day. Anything they touched would be unclean for a day.

When a couple had sex and the man ejaculated semen, they would both be unclean for the day. The bed and sheets would be unclean. All the rules were clearly laid out to keep the nation pure and undefiled. Leviticus 15 also includes a section for women who are having their monthly period.

She would be unclean each day of her period and for seven days following her last discharge. Anyone she touched or who touched her would be unclean. Anything she touched would be unclean.

SOCIAL PROBLEMS

This suffering lady not only had to endure the physical challenges of having her period, but the social ones as well. Basically she would have been under quarantine for twelve years. Going into a public place would not have been an option.

With the small streets and crowded market places, she would be inevitably touching many people. She would need to tell the crowd that she was sorry, but because of her medical problem, she was unclean and now, so were they. Very embarrassing. Very awkward. If she was married, she wouldn't be able to have sex with her husband at all. This was disallowed according to the law. This would have put great emotional stress on her, her husband, and her family. *"Do not approach a woman to have sexual relations during the uncleanness of her monthly period"* (Leviticus 18:19).

So, we know her problems. Weak, in pain, poor, embarrassed, and a social outcast.

HER REVELATION

What was it that God spoke to her? We read it clearly. *"She said to herself,*

'If I only touch his cloak, I will be healed'" (Matthew 9:21). The idea was from God. The idea brought hope to her. We don't know when, but this woman got a God-thought. It may have been weeks prior to Jesus coming to Capernaum. It may have been the very morning Jesus and his disciples were sailing to her town. Either way, it happened. A simple thought. God's thoughts are often so simple that we miss them. Remember He speaks to us as sheep; with a calm and quiet voice.

THE EXAMPLE OF NAAMAN

Do you remember Naaman the general from Aram (2 Kings 5)? The prophet Elisha tells him the secret to his breakthrough was to dip himself seven times in the Jordan river. He was angry. He expected something bold, something that required courage and honour. This was too simple. But the simple word was the key to his breakthrough. He needed to value the word. When Naaman acted on it, he was healed of leprosy. He got into the Faith Zone.

THE EXAMPLE OF ELIJAH

Do you remember Elijah running from Jezebel (1 Kings 19)? The Lord told him to go and stand on a ledge and he would pass by. A powerful wind tore the mountains apart and shattered rocks. An earthquake followed, and then a firestorm. Then came a gentle whisper. Elijah knew that God was in the big and loud experiences, but that when He spoke it would be a hushed sound. He was right.

THE EXAMPLE OF SAMUEL

Do you remember Samuel (1 Samuel 3)? In an age when the Lord rarely spoke and when people hardly received visions, God spoke to this young boy. Samuel would have missed it if he hadn't been prompted three times. Each time he heard the voice he got up from his cot and ran to Eli the priest. Eli was smart enough to recognize that the Lord was seeking to communicate with this young lad.

MY EXAMPLE

While I have heard the audible voice of the Lord only a few times, I have heard the quiet voice of the Lord tens of thousands of times. This is how He speaks to most of us most of the time. For me, it is usually a simple thought that sounds exactly like me. I think, *Don't close the car door, your keys are inside.*

This man has back pain.

Ask that person if a red flower means anything to them.

These quiet, unspectacular ideas are full of life if I value them. They are the key to my healing ministry. They are how financial breakthroughs have happened in my life. God constantly helps me to know what his heart is. He does this so that he can bless me and have me be a blessing to others.

The bleeding lady gets a simple God thought. *"If I only touch his cloak, I will be healed."* What will she do about it?

HER ACTION STEPS

We know her problem. We know her revelation. We've also read how she acted.

> *"Just then a woman who had been subject to bleeding for twelve years came up behind him and touched the edge of his cloak"* MATTHEW 9:20.

When this lady heard that Jesus was in town that day, she did exactly what God had revealed to her. She was willing to risk breaking the Levitical protocol. She joined the crowd rushing to see and touch Jesus.

Let me back up just a bit. In a later chapter we are going to talk about the parallel story that is happening at the very same time. Matthew, Mark, and Luke all tell us that a twelve-year-old girl in Capernaum is dying. Her father's name is Jairus and he is the synagogue ruler (Mark 5:22). He meets Jesus on the shore of the Sea of Galilee and begs Jesus to touch his daughter. He too has faith for a touch. *"He pleaded earnestly with him (Jesus), 'My little daughter is dying. Please come and put your hands on her so that she will be healed and live'"* (Mark 5:23).

The Bible tells us that *"Jesus went with him. A large crowd followed and pressed around him"* (Mark 5:24). This lady joined that crowd. She was the reason why Jesus never got to Jairus' home before the little girl died.

The action that this suffering woman received from the Lord was to touch the hem his garments. Most likely Jesus had tassels on his outer robes. This is what she touched. In order to get close enough to Jesus to touch his hem, she would need to be on her stomach, or her hands and knees. Picture her pushing her way under people's feet.

Each one she touches is now unclean. No one notices her. No one cares; they too are pressing in. There he is. She reaches out a hand, pushes it towards the slowly moving Jesus, and touches the hem of his clothes.

HER REWARD

Boom. Two things happened immediately.

First, she received her healing from God. She had tapped into the Faith Zone. Second, Jesus stopped walking. He knew that something miraculous had just happened. I love what happens next. It is reward time. We read about the woman's reward in all three narratives. *"And the woman was healed at that moment"* (Matthew 9:22).

Mark's narrative gives us more information: *"Immediately her bleeding stopped and she felt in her body that she was freed from her suffering"* (Mark 5:29). The bleeding that had continued for twelve years instantly stops. She feels her body improve. She is free from her suffering.

Do you remember in chapter one of this book how I said that there are two great benefits for acting in faith? Hebrews 11:6 tells us that we please God when we act on his revelation, and that he rewards us when we do. Verse 16 of the chapter tells us that God is not ashamed of us when we act on revelation and that he begins to invest in our future.

This lady got both of these that day. Faith Zone rewards.

SOMETHING HAPPENED

Jesus, knowing how his Father communicated with him, had an experience. Something great just happened. *"But Jesus said, 'Someone touched me; I know that power has gone out from me'"* (Luke 8:46). Jesus physically felt that anointing power had left his body. He felt a power surge. To him this meant that someone had just been healed.

Jesus also acted on revelation. He too stepped out in faith. *"'Who touched me?' Jesus asked"* (Luke 8:45). You know the story. The disciples remind him that everyone is touching, that everyone wants a selfie photo with Jesus. But Jesus insists that someone has received a miracle. He wants to celebrate this. Who is it?

I love what happens now. The lady reveals herself, but instead of receiving more shame, she gets a public blessing.

> *Then the woman, seeing that she could not go unnoticed, came trembling and fell at his feet. In the presence of all the people, she told why she had touched him and how she had been instantly healed.* LUKE 8:47

Perhaps with her head down she tells her full story to Jesus and to all of the citizens of Capernaum. She describes her God-thought, the action step the Lord asked her to take. *"If I only touch his cloak, I will be healed"* (Matthew 9:21). Epic. I can see the shock in the faces of some of the people. What is she doing in the crowd? She's unclean. Did she touch me? Others, the women especially, are overjoyed for her. She is free.

Mark's version gives us more insights. *"Then the woman, knowing what had happened to her, came and fell at his feet and, trembling with fear, told him the whole truth"* (Mark 5:33).

MORE REWARDS

Her reward continues. Jesus speaks to her. *"He said to her, 'Daughter, your faith has healed you. Go in peace and be freed from your suffering'"* (Mark 5:34). Two big statements from our Lord.

First, it was her faith; acting on that revelation healed her. Wow. Jesus is making a clear statement. I didn't do this miracle; she did it. I had no clue it was going to happen, but she did. She had confidence in what God spoke into her heart. In a sense, Jesus had nothing to do in this miracle. He was the object of her touch. He had no clue it was going to happen. Second, Jesus tells her to go in peace. *Shalom* is the word he speaks over her. Basically what Jesus said to her and the listening crowd is this: not only are you free from your physical suffering, but you are free from the emotional and social stigma. You are clean.

By the way, this story is important because it shows us the humanity of Jesus. While Jesus was and is fully God, he also chose not to function as God while on earth. He lived like us (Philippians 2:6–8). Jesus didn't perform one miracle or heal one person through his divinity. Every healing that took place was a result of Jesus acting in faith and relying on the anointing. I'll develop this more fully in chapter twelve.

The simplicity of how faith works is evident in this story. This lady is a role model for acting on revelation. She desperately needs a healing. She has a God-thought. She acts on it. She gets her reward: a healing. I can live like this. I get God-thoughts. I can have confidence in them. I can do what Father God says. I know God speaks to you as well. That means that if you act on His revelations, He will also reward your faith. This is what Paul spoke of when he said we are to live by faith. *"For we live by faith, not by sight"* (2 Corinthians 5:7).

ENOCH ADEBOYE'S WORD OF KNOWLEDGE

The largest church in the world today is The Redeemed Christian Church in Lagos, Nigeria. I have had the distinct privilege of meeting the pastor several times. In my opinion, he is one of God's generals.

Enoch Adeboye[1] has led this church since 1981. He is the second pastor in the church's history and under his leadership, the congregation has exploded to over one million. They have literally tens of thousands of congregations around the world and are expanding every week. Enoch is one of the humblest men I have ever met.

He has come to Toronto each summer for the last number of years. Three years in a row, I had the privilege to be involved in his Holy Ghost prayer meetings. Each time, I was the only white man on the stage, but since I grew up in Africa, I was used to it. Once I was asked to deliver the guest sermon and twice I have had the privilege of leading a prayer time for the nation of Canada.

In 2013, a miracle happened at one of these events, very similar to the story we have just looked at. Daddy G.O., as Enoch is affectionately called by his members (G.O. stands for General Overseer), ministers with great words of knowledge when he speaks. I would estimate that he gives upwards of 25 words while he preaches.

He interrupts his own sermons with statements like, "the Lord says that..." At this particular meeting he had had many words that hundreds of people could grab onto. The Nigerian tradition is if you feel the word is for you, you jump to your feet and wave a white cloth or handkerchief. For some words, hundreds stand and wave. It is awesome to see folks grabbing a word and taking the first steps of faith. By standing, they are telling those around them that this one is for me.

One of his words of knowledge was for just one person. Pastor Enoch said something like "the Lord says that there is a woman who has been bleeding like the lady with the issue of blood in the Bible. The Lord says it has stopped." Instantly, from the right side of the crowd of 14,000, a woman screamed. It was one of those blood-curdling screams that you don't easily forget. There was pain in her voice. There was desperation in her shriek. We heard chairs move as she crashed to the ground. Then the meeting continued on.

These all-night meetings start around 7:30 p.m. and are advertised to finish at 3 a.m. After many choir songs, after two or three sermons and ministry times, the meeting finishes with testimonies. A large crowd of people are usually willing to share, but the leaders narrow it down to about a dozen, who get on the stage. There are always babies that are introduced who are now two to three months old. They are the result of Pastor Enoch ministering healing to couples that were infertile at the previous year's conference.

One lady stole the show with her testimony. She confessed, "I was the woman who screamed." She told us that when the word was given, that she felt God powerfully touch her body just like the woman from Capernaum. She said she collapsed to the ground as God touched her. Then she related to us that she went to the women's restroom to check if her bleeding had stopped. It had. To say there were shouts of celebration was an understatement. Usually Enoch and his wife sit on the stage emotionless while the testimonies are shared. They have heard it all before. I remember a small smile coming to his face when this lady told us all what God had done.

Friends, God cares about us. He wants to make a way for us to receive what we need from Him. God can do miracles today. He is the same yesterday, today and tomorrow (Hebrews 13:8). I believe that He is willing to help you in your circumstances. The first step in getting your miracle is to hear His voice. Step two is to act.

Let me pray that God will speak a life-giving word to you today.

Father, thank you for simple stories such as this lady in Capernaum.
Father, thank you that we see the same pattern over and over again in

the Scriptures. People heard your voice, acted, and then you rewarded them according to their faith. Father would you speak to each one who needs a breakthrough. Reveal to them what they need to know, and what they need to do, to receive their breakthrough. We pray this in Jesus' name. Amen.

GOING DEEPER

1. What is an obstacle that you feel is hindering you? Ask the Lord what He feels about this. What does He tell you? What does He ask you to do?

2. Of the faith steps—revelation, obstacle, action, and reward—which one do you find the hardest to walk in? Ask the Lord why that is. Then ask Him to give you wisdom, strength, or whatever it is you need to make the jump to the next level.

ENDNOTE

[1]Enoch Adeboye, The Redeemed Christian Church of God, eaadeboye.com

CHAPTER 7

The Faith of the Blind Men

MATTHEW 9

As Jesus went on from there, two blind men followed him, calling out, "Have mercy on us, Son of David." When he had gone indoors, the blind men came to him, and he asked them, "Do you believe that I am able to do this?" "Yes, Lord," they replied. Then he touched their eyes and said, "According to your faith let it be done to you"; and their sight was restored. Jesus warned them sternly, "See that no one knows about this." But they went out and spread the news about him all over that region. MATTHEW 9:27-31

Perhaps one of the scariest statements Jesus made comes from this story. What Jesus says puts the burden of faith, of acting on revelation, clearly on our shoulders. The statement is this: *"According to your faith let it be done to you."*

If we use my definition of faith, acting on revelation, the statement reads like this: according to my acting on revelation let it be done to me. Perhaps a more accurate statement would be: according to the level of your acting on revelation, let it be done to you. Clearly what Jesus is saying is that we play a huge part in receiving our breakthroughs based on how we respond to what God has revealed to us. We decide. We can either agree with what God wants to do or we can negate it.

If I am like the Roman centurion and have great faith, I will see great results. If I am like the disciples with little faith, I will see little results. If I am like the people of Nazareth with no faith, I will see no results. It's really very simple isn't it? I need to be personally responding to what the Lord reveals to me. I get to choose if I enter the Faith Zone. I can't be blaming others or putting the burden for breakthroughs on the shoulders of anyone else other than myself. It is according to my acting on revelation.

This story of the two blind men who get their sight takes place in Capernaum. The story takes place within hours, perhaps minutes, of two other miracles: the lady who is healed from a twelve-year blood disorder and Jairus' twelve-year-old daughter who is raised from the dead.

A GREAT DAY IN CAPERNAUM

I love the boldness of these two men. Let me take you through what I believe happened that day.

Capernaum, as I've said already, is a town of about a thousand people. It is where Jesus based his ministry for three years. Great miracles have taken place in this town already. Earlier in the day, Twitter explodes, telling people that Jesus is coming home. Many of the people have gathered at the landing area for boats slightly south and west of the town. Jairus, a leading man in the town, has humbled himself and sought out Jesus at the water's edge.

As Jesus makes his way to Jairus' home, the crowds increase. Walking through this town would not have taken long. When the streets are empty, it is a minute's walk from east to west, or north to south. The problem though is getting to the home. The streets are narrow and the public spaces are outside the town. The market area would be where most people congregated during the daylight hours. As Jesus comes into the town, he passes through this busy area. As Jesus is walking, smiling, and talking to his friends, he stops suddenly.

MIRACLE ONE—WOMAN BLEEDING FOR 12 YEARS

Someone has just been healed. He knows it. Jesus stops, much to the consternation of Jairus, who is trying to rush Jesus to his home. It turns out that one of the ladies from town just had a life-changing healing. As Jesus ministers to this lady, as the people listen to her story, as the town folk celebrate with her, a couple people approach Jairus with very bad news. His daughter has died.

MIRACLE TWO—GIRL RAISED TO LIFE

Jesus confronts this news with a bold statement to *"just believe."* Jesus then tells the crowd to stay put and continue celebrating with the newly healed woman. Jesus, Jairus and his two friends, plus Peter, James, and John, make their way to Jairus' home. Not everyone has been in the market that day. Some, probably family members and close friends, have been holding a vigil outside of Jairus' home. When the girl dies, the prayers turn into mourning. The sound of wailing greets Jairus and Jesus as they approach.

After a short confrontation with the mourning group, Jesus goes into the small home with the girl's parents plus three of his disciples. A miracle takes place. The little girl is alive. Jesus asks the parents to keep this their secret, but how could they not tell people? I can imagine the immense joy in this home. Family would find out, then friends, and soon the news would quickly spread around the town. Capernaum is a happy town today. Two great miracles in one day.

MIRACLE THREE — TWO BLIND MEN

Somewhere in the town are two blind men. At some point in the day they hear what has transpired. Perhaps they were begging in the market area and heard about the lady who was healed of her blood disorder. Wherever they were, they made a decision. If everyone is getting his or her miracle today, we need ours.

The text tells us that Jesus went indoors to relax. The blind men follow, but with no apparent invitation. A home invasion.

DID JESUS OWN A HOUSE?

Let's speculate about this house. Whose house was it?

Is it possible that this is the home where Jesus stays while in Capernaum?

Is it possible that the two blind men know where Jesus lives?

Is it possible that the home belongs to Jesus?

Mark 2:15 tells us something very interesting. Mark, who is writing his narrative based on the accounts of Peter, tells us that Jesus had a house. We know that Peter lived in Capernaum, so out of the all disciples he would be the one to know.

The New International Version makes an assumption and probably mistranslates this verse because of it. I believe that the translators assumed that if Jesus said, "*foxes have dens and birds have nests, but the Son of Man has no place to lay his head*" (Matthew 8:20), that the home had to be someone else's. Here is what Mark writes, according to the NIV translation: "*While Jesus was having dinner at Levi's house, many tax collectors and sinners were eating with him and his disciples, for there were many who followed him*" (Mark 2:15).

But here is how the King James Version translates the passage: "*And it came to pass, that, as Jesus sat at meat in his house, many publicans and sinners sat also together with Jesus and his disciples: for there were many, and they followed him.*" (Mark 2:15 KJV)

And one more from the New American Standard Bible. "*And it happened that He was reclining at the table in his house, and many tax collectors and sinners were dining with Jesus and His disciples; for there were many of them, and they were following Him.*" (Mark 2:15 NASB)

So, let's assume therefore, that Jesus did have a home in Capernaum. It is quite possible that this is where these two blind men come for their miracle. Jesus has had a busy day and needs to relax. He heads home to catch up on his emails and post some photos on Instagram.

> *When he had gone indoors, the blind men came to him, and he asked them, "Do you believe that I am able to do this?" "Yes, Lord," they replied.*
> MATTHEW 9:28

I love the nonchalant conversation that Jesus has with these two men. We clearly don't have the full narrative, rather the short version. From reading between the lines, I am going to guess what happened.

The two men enter Jesus' home and are standing at the door with their white canes. Jesus probably greets them by name. They say something like, "Is it true that a woman was healed in the market today?"
"Yes."
"Is it true that Jairus' daughter died and was raised back to life?"
"Yes."
"We want to be healed too."
"Do you believe that I am able to do this?"
"Yes, Lord," they reply.

Jesus then does what he always does when he sees people acting on revelation—he responds positively. He touches the eyes of the men and says a simple command. *"Then he touched their eyes and said, 'According to your faith let it be done to you'; and their sight was restored"* (Matthew 9:29-30).

WHO STARTED THE MIRACLE?

Let me ask you a question: Did Jesus initiate the miracle or did the miracle occur because of their faith? They entered the Faith Zone. Jesus responded to *their* faith.

I hope that as we read these stories from Matthew's gospel you are seeing a pattern. Yes, there are clearly times when Jesus is led by his Father to minister. But there is also a number of stories where Jesus has no clue what is about to take place, rather he responds to the faith of others.

Jesus did not know that a bleeding lady was going to touch him and receive her healing. Jesus did not know that Jairus would meet him at the shore that morning. Jesus did not know that four men would lower a paralyzed man through a roof.

Back to the possibility of Jesus having a home in this town. I'd like you to take one more look at the story of the four friends and their attempt to take their lame friend to Jesus. I believe that the home that had the roof ripped off may have been Jesus' home.

We know that Jesus lived in Capernaum. We know that the people would have known where he lived. As I read the text again, it is very probable that this story takes place at Jesus' home.

A few days later, when Jesus again entered Capernaum, the people heard that he had come home. They gathered in such large numbers that there was no room left, not even outside the door, and he preached the word to them. Some men came, bringing to him a paralyzed man, carried by four of them. Since they could not get him to Jesus because of the crowd, they made an opening in the roof above Jesus by digging through it and then lowered the mat the man was lying on. When Jesus saw their faith, he said to the paralyzed man, "Son, your sins are forgiven." **MARK 2:1-5**

Two reason for my guess. First is the phrase *he had come home.* Is this simply referring to he came back to Capernaum or is it back to his own home in Capernaum? The second reason I believe this is Jesus' home is that there is no mention of a homeowner reacting to his roof collapsing. We know that Jesus would forgive, but I'm not sure that others would. I realize this is an argument from silence. I can't prove that the home was Jesus' nor can others prove me wrong. When we get to heaven, we'll see who's right.

Let's move on and go back to the two blind men. We need to explore two key points.

First, the question Jesus asked them.
Second, Jesus' statement as to how the miracle took place.

WHAT DOES IT MEAN TO BELIEVE?

Let's talk a bit about what it means to believe. *"He (Jesus) asked them, 'Do you believe that I am able to do this?' 'Yes, Lord,' they replied"* (Matthew 9:28). To believe is to trust that what you are hearing and seeing is accurate. It is to have confidence in what you know to be true. Sounds a lot like the definition of faith from Hebrews 11:1: "*Now faith is confidence in what we hope for and assurance about what we do not see.*"

Let's take a look at a few other statements from Jesus on belief.

> "*If you believe, you will receive whatever you ask for in prayer.*" MATTHEW 21:22

> "*For John (the baptizer) came to you to show you the way of righteousness, and you did not believe him, but the tax collectors and the prostitutes did. And even after you saw this, you did not repent and believe him.*" MATTHEW 21:32

Believing and faith are basically the same thing. They are a response to knowing something. We've had a revelation of something and we agree. Faith is simply the acting out of the revelation.

The opposite of faith is fear. Our challenge when we have a God-thought is to hold onto it even when Satan challenges its validity. It is normal for us to have this kind of struggle. People in Jesus' day had difficulties as well.

> *Overhearing what they said (to Jairus), Jesus told him, "Don't be afraid; just believe.*" MARK 5:36

> *Immediately the boy's father exclaimed, "I do believe; help me overcome my unbelief.*" MARK 9:34

So, believing is all about holding onto the conviction that our revelations are truthful and correct. The question now is, what do we do with those revelations?

WERE THESE THE FIRST PEOPLE
HEALED OF BLINDNESS?

The two blind men in Jesus' home believed that Jesus could help them. This is a big deal. Let me tell you why. It is hard to know for certain who was the first person to regain their sight, for several reasons. The Bible doesn't record all the stories of Jesus healing people, nor do we have a definitive chronology of his healings.

Having said that, it is very possible that these two guys were the very first ones in the history of mankind to receive their sight. There are simply no stories of people getting their eyesight restored before this. God had promised the ancients that it would happen, but it hadn't yet. That is, until Jesus brought the kingdom of God to earth and new rules took effect.

In that day the deaf will hear the words of the scroll, and out of gloom and darkness the eyes of the blind will see. ISAIAH 29:18

Then will the eyes of the blind be opened and the ears of the deaf unstopped. ISAIAH 35:5

Jews today believe the Messiah will do three miracles when he returns: open the eyes of the blind, free people from a demon, and raise a dead person after three days. Jesus already performed all three. Even if these men were not the first ones to be healed of blindness, for them to state that they believed in the possibility of the healing was huge. No one had ever been healed of blindness. It was the impossible miracle.

But they believed it was possible. This is where faith kicks in. After they affirm their belief that a miracle could happen; Jesus touches their eyes. Boom, it happens. Then Jesus tells them why it happened. It happened because of their faith. By acting on their revelation, they received a great reward.

> *"Do you believe that I am able to do this?"*
> *"Yes, Lord," they replied. Then he touched their eyes and said,*
> *"According to your faith let it be done to you"; and their sight was restored.*
> MATTHEW 9:28-30

FORMULA FOR MIRACLES

Let's review again so we don't miss how easy it is to get breakthroughs.

These two unnamed men had a revelation. It appears to be a very simple one; Jesus can restore their sight. Their action step was also simple. They went to Jesus' home because they knew he was in town that day. They marched in and asked Jesus to help them. Jesus, always eager to respond to the faith of others, did his part. He clarified that they were eligible for their miracles when He asked them what they believed. Jesus was comfortable with how they replied, so he touched them. At that moment their blind eyes opened.

Remember the formula that the Bible sets out for us. It is simple and yet it takes our cooperation. We hear, we act, and we get a reward from our Father in heaven. This is how the Faith Zone operates.

BLIND FIRSTS IN HISTORY

History records some interesting facts relating to blindness.

1784: The first "school for the blind" was established in France. Before long, schools like this were established in England and throughout Europe.

1809: Louis Braille was born in France. He developed his tactile reading and writing system by 1820.[1]

1905: The first cornea transplant was performed by Eduard Zirm (Olomouc Eye Clinic, now in Czech Republic). It is one of the first types of transplant surgery successfully performed.[2]

1969: On April 22 doctors at Methodist hospital in Houston, Texas, managed to perform what was called the first human eye transplant on John Madden. The operation, while a first, was not successful in returning Mr. Madden's eyesight.[3]

Human technology and medical advancement for blindness are way behind the good news of God's kingdom. Somewhere about AD 27–30, news spread throughout Israel that Jesus of Nazareth was opening the eyes of the blind simply by touching them. Two millennia later; technology begins to catch up to what Jesus did.

BLIND EYE IN SCOTLAND

In July of 2014, Sandra and I went on a speaking tour at the Elim Pentecostal churches in the United Kingdom. Our second night was in Paisley, Scotland at a church led by Tom Paton. We had a ministry time following my talk. Most of the time I prefer to lead ministry in the seats rather than do the ministry myself. If I do the ministry people will leave the meeting talking about how Steve Long did this miracle or that healing. That makes me feel good, but I prefer the people to leave knowing that it was their prayer for the sick person sitting next to them that worked. This empowers people in the congregation to know that God uses their prayers and it grows their expectation to see more of the miraculous.

This particular night we had folks who needed a healing stand up. We matched people together and had them pronounce healing over the person needing a breakthrough.

My healing belongs to me because of what Jesus has done. I receive my healing now.

Then came the fun part, where we checked to see what God had done. Several people put up their hands to indicate that something good had happened. One of them was Jim. Jim told us that he was completely blind in one of his eyes. He had no sight at all. No flashes of light, no colors, nothing. Well, that changed!

Jim told us that after his friends prayed for him, he could see lights. Because he was in the midst of receiving his healing, we had everyone continue to pray for him. Thirty seconds later, he could see images. One minute later he could see colours. After three or four rounds, Jim was able to read from a large-print Bible.

A lady sitting two chairs over from Jim also had a healing that night. She had a large thyroid growth on her neck the size of a golf ball. It completely disappeared! She had always worn blouses with high collars to cover herself and to hide the tumour. She was thrilled with her healing. Turns out that she was Jim's wife.

Why do healings like this occur? Two simple reasons. First, people believe that God is still in the healing and miracle business. Second, people enter the Faith Zone by coming to a healing meeting, by standing when an invitation is given, by letting friends place their hands on them, and letting them say a prayer. God then rewards them according to their faith.

Clearly God is the one responsible for the miracles, but you and I get to partner with him. When we agree with Him, we become eligible for our breakthroughs. Believing God is shown through our agreement. Faith is proven when we act on what we know to be true.

God rewards these types of people. Let's say this prayer together.

> *Father I want to partner with you. I want to be led by your Spirit. I want to begin to live in the Faith Zone. Help me to honour you when you speak to me. Help me to value the ideas, thoughts and insights that you are giving me. Help me to be bold when it comes to believing. Help me not to waiver. Help me to enter into all that you have for me. May I be used by you to bless others. In Jesus' name, Amen.*

GOING DEEPER

1. A father asked Jesus to help him with his faith, to take away his unbelief. What is an issue in your life that having faith for seems impossible? Ask Jesus what he wants to say to you about this? Record what he says to you.

2. The phrase *according to your faith* has positive and negative implications. Ask the Lord to remind you of something in the past that you didn't have faith for. Ask the Lord to give you a second chance so you can move it into the positive realm. What does he want you to believe today concerning that? Write it down. Speak it out. Renounce all doubt as lies from the enemy.

ENDNOTES

[1] James Omvig, *History of Blindness* (retrieved December 2015) https://www.actionfund.org/history-blindness

[2] Wikipedia, *Corneal Transplantation* (retrieved December 2015) http://en.wikipedia.org/wiki/Corneal_transplantation

[3] Sharon O'Brien, *Science and Technology milestones in 1969* (retrieved December 2015) http://seniorliving.about.com/od/boomernostalgia/tp/1969-milestones-science.htm

CHAPTER 8

The City Without Faith

MATTHEW 13

Coming to his hometown, he began teaching the people in their synagogue, and they were amazed. "Where did this man get this wisdom and these miraculous powers?" they asked. "Isn't this the carpenter's son? Isn't his mother's name Mary, and aren't his brothers James, Joseph, Simon and Judas? Aren't all his sisters with us? Where then did this man get all these things?" And they took offence at him. But Jesus said to them, "A prophet is not without honor except in his own town and in his own home." And he did not do many miracles there because of their lack of faith. MATTHEW 13:54-58

One of the absolute best novels of all time is *A Tale of Two Cities*. Charles Dickens wrote the book in 1859. The story unfolded weekly via a newspaper over eight months. This novel ranks as the third most popular selling book of all time (200 million) behind Don Quixote (300 million) and the Bible (5 billion). *A Tale of Two Cities* is the story of Paris and London. Paris struggles during the revolutionary years. Death, fear, and poverty are rampant. Meanwhile, London has none of the violence and hardship. The book is a classic.

In this chapter we will look at two towns: the towns of Nazareth and Capernaum. One town sees miracles while the other doesn't. How is this possible? The title of the chapter says it all: no faith.

The Bible tells us that all things are possible for Father God (Matthew 19:26). Our Father is able to do anything that He sees fit. He is invincible. He is all-powerful. He can override any rule of the universe whenever He pleases. Do you agree? Most of us do, as this is what the Bible teaches over and over again. Yet in spite of what we know about God, we often don't believe that God can help us with our problems and challenges.

As a full-time pastor since 1981, I have heard thousands of stories. I have prayed and laid hands on more than three hundred thousand people in my time as a revivalist. In the course of ministering to people, many people have told me that God can't help them. Everything in me has to be restrained when I hear this. Sandra tells me that sometimes my body actually shakes. She can see that my spirit is so upset that my physical body reacts.

You may be reading this chapter and thinking to yourself, *Hold on now, my circumstances are unique.*
My parents had faith and they never saw their breakthrough.
My experience is that God hasn't helped me.

This may be true of your experiences, but I don't believe that experiences always reflects what God wants. If you will allow me, I'd like to use the Bible as my foundation to share with you one of the most shocking stories in the life of Jesus.

NAZARETH

Nazareth is a town, where the people actually stopped the will of God. They did something that hindered the breakthrough anointing that Jesus carried. Jesus wanted to do miracles in his hometown of Nazareth, but the people wouldn't let him.

Nazareth is the town where Jesus grew up. He moved to Nazareth when his family came back from Egypt (Matthew 2:19-23). We don't know his exact age, but Jesus would have been a child, perhaps four or five years of age. The narrative in Luke tells us that Joseph and Mary both lived in Nazareth prior to getting married.

In the sixth month of Elizabeth's pregnancy, God sent the angel Gabriel to Nazareth, a town in Galilee, to a virgin pledged to be married to a man named Joseph, a descendant of David. The virgin's name was Mary. LUKE 1:26-27.

Mary and Joseph went to Bethlehem as a married couple for the Roman census, which is where Jesus was born. The texts are slightly unclear as to when the family permanently moved to Bethlehem. Once Jesus was dedicated in the temple (Luke 2:22-38), it would appear that the family moved back to Nazareth for a very short period of time. Perhaps long enough to pack their bags and relocate to Bethlehem. The other option is that the following passage from Luke 2 is a general overview of the early life of Jesus. It skips his years in Egypt and simply jumps to when Jesus returns to Nazareth.

When Joseph and Mary had done everything required by the Law of the Lord, they returned to Galilee to their own town of Nazareth. And the child grew and became strong; he was filled with wisdom, and the grace of God was on him. LUKE 2:39-40

What we do know is that Jesus and his parents are living in a house in Bethlehem when the Magi arrived. The Greek word to describe Jesus is toddler, not baby. We also know that Jesus was about two years of age, as this is the grouping that Herod the Great had killed. While we don't know the exact date that Jesus was born, we do know the exact date when the Magi visited Mary, Joseph, and Jesus in Bethlehem. The research in the documentary *The Star of Bethlehem*,[1] including NASA's Starry Night computer program, has dated when the miracle star stood still.

That day is December 25, 2 BC. This is one of the reasons why Christians celebrate the Lord's birth on Christmas Day. It is also true that December 25 was a Roman holiday and a statutory holiday, even for slaves. History makes it clear that followers of Jesus chose this day to remember the birth of Jesus.

It would appear from Matthew's narrative that Joseph had a dream that night warning him that great danger was ahead. He was to flee at once to Egypt. He does, without even waiting until morning (Matthew 2:13-15).

Fast forward to when Jesus is growing up in Nazareth. His father Joseph is called the carpenter, or more literally, the builder. We are not sure whether he is a house framer, builds cabinets, or furniture (Matthew 13:55). Nazareth is in the north of Galilee and was an obscure village. There is no mention of this town in the Old Testament. When Philip talks to Nathanael about Jesus, Nathanael's view is that nothing good comes from that town, which was very prophetic (John 1:46).

Nazareth, however, was the place where a teenage virgin named Mary lived. Gabriel, one of the messenger angels, visited her with the incredible news that she would be the mother of the Messiah (Luke 1:26–27). God visited this town at least once. We empathize with Mary and Joseph and the trauma they must have gone through as they tried to explain how Mary got pregnant before they were officially married (Matthew 1:18–19).

RUMORS OF ILLEGITIMACY IN NAZARETH

The rumors were out that Mary was carrying another man's child. Joseph also believed this until an angel corrected him (Matthew 1:20–25). In fact, some of the slurs against Jesus while he ministered as an adult were directly aimed at his birthright. In John 9, the religious leaders taunt Jesus by saying they don't know where he is from. Everyone knew Jesus was from Nazareth. They were inferring that Jesus was a bastard.

> Then they hurled insults at him and said, "You are this fellow's disciple. We are disciples of Moses. We know that God spoke to Moses, but as for this fellow, we don't even know where he comes from." JOHN 9:28–29

One of the reasons Joseph and Mary may have moved from Nazareth to Bethlehem was to escape the gossip and innuendoes about Mary's pregnancy. Now five years later, they are back. They try to settle down and raise a growing family.

Every year a group from every town would make their way to Jerusalem for the Passover. This journey for those from Nazareth would take up to three

weeks. The town's people would travel together for safety and companion-
ship. These pilgrimages up to Jerusalem would be highly anticipated. Twelve-
year-old boys would be allowed to make the journey for the first time.

When Jesus turns twelve and becomes a man by Jewish tradition, he too
makes this trek with his mom and dad. If you haven't read the narrative,
please take time to read Luke 2:41–50. On the journey home, Mary and
Joseph discover that their son is not in their tour group. Panic sets in and
they rush back to Jerusalem. They find Jesus lecturing the religious leaders. It is the first time we see that Jesus knew that the primary name of
God is *Father*. He would later use that term almost three hundred times.
"Why were you searching for me?" he asked. *"Didn't you know I had to be in
my Father's house?"* (Luke 2:49).

I'm sure the good people of Nazareth heard how Joseph and Mary left
Jesus behind. The incident wasn't funny, like the comedy movie *Home
Alone*; this was more dramatic.

Then there is silence for eighteen years. We hear nothing of Jesus until
he joined other pilgrims at the Jordan River for the revival meetings led by
John the Baptizer. Jesus' ministry was launched from that moment.

JESUS' FAMILY

What we do know or can at least speculate is that Joseph died at some
point in these eighteen years. There is no record of him in the narratives of
Jesus. We also know that Mary and Joseph had other children. The Bible

mentions the siblings of Jesus. Two of them authored books in the Bible, James (the Greek text calls him Jacob)[2] and Judas, who wrote the book of Jude. James would become the first pastor of the church in Jerusalem.[3]

> Isn't this the carpenter's son? Isn't his mother's name Mary, and aren't his brothers James, Joseph, Simon and Judas? Aren't all his sisters with us?
> MATTHEW 13:55-56

Mary and her children are not quite sure about the ministry of Jesus, at least in his early days. Jesus' sharp comments about who he considered family may hint that his brothers were opposed to him (Matthew 12:46-48).

Let's jump forward to the story that I want to focus on.

Did you know that there was one attitude, one mindset, one thought, that stopped Jesus from performing miracles in Nazareth? The phrases used by Matthew and Mark are slightly different and yet the same. Jesus wants to do miracles in his hometown, yet he can't. Why?

Lack of faith.

Let's read the two accounts.

> Coming to his hometown, he began teaching the people in their synagogue, and they were amazed. "Where did this man get this wisdom and these miraculous powers?" they asked. "Isn't this the carpenter's son? Isn't his mother's name Mary, and aren't his brothers James, Joseph, Simon and Judas? Aren't all his sisters with us? Where then did this man get all these things?" And they

took offence at him. But Jesus said to them, "A prophet is not without honor except in his own town and in his own home." And he did not do many miracles there because of their lack of faith. MATTHEW 13:54-58

Jesus left there and went to his hometown, accompanied by his disciples. When the Sabbath came, he began to teach in the synagogue, and many who heard him were amazed. "Where did this man get these things?" they asked. "What's this wisdom that has been given him? What are these remarkable miracles he is performing? Isn't this the carpenter? Isn't this Mary's son and the brother of James, Joseph, Judas and Simon? Aren't his sisters here with us?" And they took offence at him. Jesus said to them, "A prophet is not without honor except in his own town, among his relatives and in his own home." He could not do any miracles there, except lay his hands on a few sick people and heal them. He was amazed at their lack of faith. MARK 6:1-6

In an earlier story of Jesus in Nazareth, which we will get to later, there is an interesting phrase that talks about this synagogue: *"He went to Nazareth, where he had been brought up, and on the Sabbath day he went into the synagogue, as was his custom"* (Luke 4:16).

As was his custom. This tells us that Jesus attended this synagogue faithfully until he moved to Capernaum. There was only one synagogue in Nazareth. If you take a tour to Israel, you can sit in that synagogue. Nazareth today is a city of 210,000. It is mostly Arabs, with some Jews and some Christians. In Jesus' day the population would be approximately 1,800. Everyone would have been Jewish. Everyone would have attended this synagogue unless they had been excommunicated. That was very rare.

JESUS' FIRST RECORDED SERMON WAS IN NAZARETH

So when Jesus is invited to share at his "home" church after an absence of a few years; I believe this is a big deal. Why? Because the last time he was there the people tried to kill him.

Luke 4 tells us that Jesus went to the revival meetings led by John the Baptizer. My guess is that he joined a group similar to those who would be travelling to the Passover. But Jesus didn't come back with them. Several of the narratives tell us that when Jesus was baptized, he was transported into the desert (Mark 1:12). Mind you, the desert was just steps away from where he was baptized. You can visit the site today, slightly east of Jericho. In years past, this area was a military zone, but today it is a tourist destination in the middle of a land mine zone.

Jesus doesn't return to Nazareth with his revival tour group. They have no clue where he is. Forty days later, the Bible tells us that He was now full of the Spirit. He begins to make his way home to Nazareth (Luke 4:14). Jesus quickly builds a reputation as a great teacher (Luke 4:15). So, when Jesus gets back to Nazareth, a month and half late, everyone wants to know why. They have heard that he has started a teaching ministry. A strange transition for a builder's son.

When the first Sabbath arrives, Jesus is invited to speak. What he shares is fascinating. He turns to Isaiah 61 and reads the passage about the purposes of the anointing.

> *The Spirit of the Lord is on me, because he has anointed me to proclaim good*
> *news to the poor. He has sent me to proclaim freedom for the prisoners and*
> *recovery of sight for the blind, to set the oppressed free, to proclaim the year*
> *of the Lord's favor.* LUKE 4:18-19

After standing and reading the Scriptures, he sat down. This was the custom for the sermon time. He pauses, looks around at all the people he knows. Most are those he has known all his life.

His sermon is very short: *"Today this Scripture is fulfilled in your hearing"* (Luke 4:21).

"This happened to me," is what Jesus says. I was anointed at the revival meetings. I can do all of these anointed things now. I'm sure there was a bit more to the talk than just that one line, but it was a great, to-the-point sermon.

His sermon did two things: it caused the people to marvel at his speaking abilities and his insights into the Scriptures. Perhaps some remembered when Jesus was twelve and debating the scholars in Jerusalem. The passage also tells us that the people were furious with him. I believe there were two reasons for this.

First, when he quoted the Isaiah 61 passage, Jesus ad-libbed. He added a phrase that was not in the text. He added the bit about *recovery of sight for the blind*. While this may not seem to be a big deal to you, it was to the Jews. I mentioned in the prior chapter that the Jews believed that only the Messiah would be able to open blind eyes.

The second reason for their fury was because Jesus reminded them of bad times in their history. He talked about how Gentiles received break-throughs in the past while Jews didn't (Luke 4:23-27). They took offence. The implication was that they were worse than "dogs." They felt that Jesus was talking down to them and berating them.

JESUS OFFENDS HIS HOMETOWN

Their rage turned nasty. His own church family, his hometown, his neigh-bours, and friends of the family decide to kill him. The insult they felt and the heresy they heard demanded that Jesus die, immediately. The Bible tells us that they tried to take him to the edge of the cliff (another tourist site) to throw him over, and then stone him. *"They got up, drove him out of the town, and took him to the brow of the hill on which the town was built, in order to throw him off the cliff"* (Luke 4:29).

However, Jesus somehow escapes (Luke 4:30).

You know it's time to relocate when your hometown wants you dead. So Jesus moved to Capernaum, perhaps owning his own home there. At the very least he made Capernaum his headquarters. After a few years of teaching, healing, and performing signs and wonders, Jesus went back to Nazareth. I'm sure the local promoter was expecting a full house. I'm confident that everyone in Nazareth knew that Jesus was making a comeback.

What would happen this time?

Well, nothing happened. *"He could not do any miracles there, except lay his hands on a few sick people and heal them. He was amazed at their lack of faith"* (Mark 6:5-6). Jesus could not do any miracles because of the people of Nazareth. They were the ones who stopped what God wanted to accomplish that day.

I'm sure many people needed a healing. There would have been those who needed a financial breakthrough. Everyone needed something from God. But only a few people got anything. Why? Lack of faith.

LACK OF FAITH

Three points, if I may, on this phrase.

First, lack of faith implies no faith. The people had no revelation regarding Jesus to give them hope. What they did have was amazement. They heard the stories of the miracles, but they couldn't put together that those events were possible through Jesus. No revelation.

> *Coming to his hometown, he began teaching the people in their synagogue, and they were amazed. "Where did this man get this wisdom and these miraculous powers?" they asked.* MATTHEW 13:54

Second, doubt steals the hope that leads to faith. The connotation is that fear has so enveloped the people that instead of any optimism about Jesus coming to town, they react with pessimism. Doubt is the first step towards fear. Doubt questions rather than hopes. The people were skeptical of the stories of Jesus.

Third, the people of Nazareth made a choice to not believe. Believing is the process of receiving truth. Unbelief is a willful choice to say no. It is an opposing voice to what others know to be true and right.

Another factor in this scenario is **dishonor.** Jesus pointed out that their honour was low because their expectation was low. When we don't honour what God has put in and on someone, we can't receive what they carry. We simply receive from the natural realm, a dynamic which we've already seen. Nazareth apparently was full of people who lacked faith. Their reputation of *"nothing good comes from there"* was well earned (John 1:46).

NAIN, LABRADOR

Nain is considered the suicide capital of Canada. This small town of a thousand is situated in one of the most remote regions of Canada, in Labrador. Most Canadians would have no clue where this town is, or have even heard of it. It is impoverished. It is remote. The weather conditions are harsh. You can't get there quickly and you can't get away easily. There are no roads in and out; planes are the only way to travel. When circumstances like poverty prevail, social issues follow. Nain has a high level of alcoholism. Teen pregnancies are normative. Petty crime is rampant. There is no hope.

Our church, like several others, has sown into this town. Several years ago we provided Christmas for this town. Bill and Gwen Prankard[4] organized a transport plane to bring gifts, turkeys, and food for every family in this town. We helped to cover the salary of a pastor to move to Nain. A church is now open, seeking to bring hope and to change the spiritual atmosphere. Our church didn't want Nain to be like Nazareth.

It would appear that Nazareth somehow got to the place where they had given up. They had no expectation that Jesus, their most famous citizen, could do anything. Jesus tried his best, but their response blocked the anointing on his life. This is shocking to me in two regards.

First, you and I can limit the breakthroughs that God wants to bring. Our doubt stops the anointing. Doubt is the only thing mentioned in the Bible that was able to slow down Jesus.

Second, Nazareth's lack of faith is shocking because of what had happened the week prior in Capernaum.

ONE DAY IN CAPERNAUM — MIRACLES

I want you to look at Mark 6:1-2: *"Jesus left there (Capernaum) and went to his hometown (Nazareth), accompanied by his disciples. When the Sabbath came, he began to teach in the synagogue."*

Do you see the phrase *when the Sabbath came?* That means that Nazareth's negative response occurred within one week of something. What was it that occurred the prior week in Capernaum? Glad you asked. Let me recap. We've looked at most of these stories already, but you may not have realized the significance of them as a group.

It would appear that all of what I am about to share happened on one day. Within seven days of these healings and miracles, Jesus would be back in Nazareth.

First, Jairus finds Jesus at the coast of the Galilee. He convinces Jesus to come to his home and heal his twelve-year-old daughter (Matthew 9). Jesus goes with him and is interrupted by the crowd and by a woman who gets her healing. That woman is the lady who has been bleeding for twelve years. You will remember the story, how Jesus stops when he knew that one of the people touching him has had a breakthrough (Matthew 9).

As this healing concluded, two men came to Jairus with the terrible news that his daughter is dead. Jesus says, *"Don't be afraid; just believe"* (Mark 5:36). They go to the house and Jesus raises the first of his three recorded people from the dead.

Matthew 9 tells us that Jesus then went into a home, possibly his own. Two blind men enter the home and come out with full vision. The people of Capernaum then send in a mute man and he gets his healing. All these stories happened on one day. Amazing!

ONE DAY IN NAZARETH—NOTHING

What is shocking and a bit terrifying is that within one week of Jesus' big day out in Capernaum, the next large town to the east does not believe that anything miraculous can happen. How is this possible?

The passage tells us that they knew what had just transpired in Capernaum. *"'Where did this man get this wisdom and these miraculous powers?' they asked"* (Matthew 13:54). Raising someone from the dead doesn't go unnoticed. Yet somehow the good people of Nazareth doubt that any of it happened. They don't believe the stories from the prior week.

If I was the promoter of this return visit of Jesus in Nazareth, I would be ecstatic that miracles happened the week prior. How good is that? What better way to get a full house than to have your meeting within a week of the first resurrection in over eight hundred years? But the people of Nazareth doubt and disbelieve. Is it possible that people can minimalize proven miracles? Yes. I used to do it.

HISTORY OF UNBELIEF

My upbringing was that of a missionary kid in Malawi, Africa. My parents met there. I lived in a little village called Chididi until I was five. We moved to Canada after a brief stop in England, and I've lived the rest of my life in this great nation.

My dad finished his Bible school degree and began to pastor within a Baptist denomination. I grew up conservative evangelical. What that means is that I grew up saying that I believed all the stories of the Bible, but I didn't believe that any of them could be repeated today. My expectation for miracles was minimal. God can do miracles, but He rarely does. God can heal, but for some reason He usually doesn't. My optimism was low.

Circular thinking kicks in when you grow up like I did. I was taught that God used to do miracles, they are in the Bible. But today we are in the "church age" where the miraculous and where healings don't happen. Because of what I was taught, I never expected miracles, nor did I ever pray actively for breakthroughs. Because I never expected miracles, I never saw them. I was living in the negative side of *"according to your faith be it done unto you."*

Nothing was happening, which proved what I was taught: God can, but doesn't, do miracles today.

So when I would hear that someone was healed, I would be skeptical. If some well-meaning but delusional person talked about a miracle, we smiled. We knew better. If we heard that somewhere a person was raised from the dead, we wanted evidence. If there is no death certificate, how do we know they were dead?

Well as it turns out God wants us to live by faith, not by X-rays and death certificates from qualified doctors. Faith is not about having all the facts in front of you. Faith is hearing a quiet whisper in your spirit and knowing that God is communicating to you about something He wants to do. Faith is acting on the revelation you received. It is proving to yourself that you were right, even if others disbelieve. Even if your family thinks you're a fool for hoping in the impossible.

REJECTING MY OWN PREACHING

I remember preaching a month long series at one of the Baptist churches where I was associate pastor. The title was *Why Miracles Don't Happen Today*. Very inspirational if you needed a breakthrough. Not!

The Vineyard churches were new in Canada and, to my disappointment, there was one by the airport in Toronto. They believed that healing could take place on demand. They taught that miracles were still possible. That church is the one that my wife Sandra and I now lead. I was asked by my senior pastor at the Baptist church to counteract the teaching of people like John Arnott and John Wimber. And I did. I did my research and presented proof texts to show our congregation that we should not expect miracles and breakthroughs.

The irony of this was that my sermon series was at our Wednesday night prayer meeting. So right after my thirty-minute talk we would share prayer requests. I would flip from teaching that we can't get miracles, to asking people if they needed God to do something for them? No wonder we never saw miracles and healings at our church. In hindsight I was preaching doubt and unbelief. I was convincing people who loved God that God was on vacation. God wouldn't be back to doing the miraculous until the events in the book of Revelation kicked in. (But we hoped not in our lifetime.)

Sandra and I experienced a massive transition in 1994. On January 28, 1994, we went to the revival at the Airport Vineyard and encountered the Holy Spirit for the first time. On February 4 I was loaned by our Baptist church to help administrate the revival meetings at what is now Catch The Fire Toronto. In June we officially joined John and Carol Arnott as part of their full-time staff.

At some point that summer, the Lord spoke to me through Marc Dupont. Marc was on the leadership team and functioned as the house prophet. I remember Marc talking at one of the pastors' days about those of us who had taught our people that God didn't do miracles. He encouraged us to repent from that. I did. I was reminded by the Lord of my preaching series that miracles don't happen today. I determined to make it right.

I called the man who was now leading our former church. I knew him well as we had been in Bible school together. I explained to him that God had convicted me that my sermon series some five-years prior was not what I believed now. I asked if it was possible for me to either come back on a Wednesday to recant, or at the least to have him read a rebuttal state-ment from me. He brought great relief to me by saying something funny. He said, "I don't think that many people actually listened to your talks." We both laughed knowing that to be very true. I felt better, and he did read my letter aloud.

So I do know how the good people of Nazareth could stop the anointing that Jesus carried. Jesus wanted to do miracles. Their doubt and unbelief is what stopped a potentially great revival from beginning in that city. Did people in that city need a miracle? Obviously. Did people need to be healed? Of course. So why did they doubt?

WHERE DOES DOUBT COME FROM?

I believe that doubt and unbelief come from many sources.

We doubt because our parents doubted. It's how we think, how we've grown up.
We don't believe in the miraculous because we haven't experienced it ourselves.
We quench revival because we feel that if God were to do something He would start with us, and in our church, not somewhere else.
We doubt when we are too familiar with the person whom God is using.

Jesus was in his hometown. They only had faith in His carpentry skills, not His anointing for miracles.

We don't believe because our theology says God can't do miracles in this dispensation.

We lack faith because our culture is all about visual proof.

There are a multitude of other sources. But the tragedy is that one of them, any of them, will keep us from what God our Father wants to do in our lives and the lives of our family and friends. I never want to be the reason God isn't able to do what He wants to do.

One week before Jesus was in Nazareth, great healings and miracles took place.

A twelve-year-old was raised from the dead.

A lady was healed from a terrible blood condition, which had been with her for twelve years and was getting worse.

Two men who were blind were able to see within minutes of invading a home and connecting with Jesus.

A mute man was instantly set free with one touch from Jesus.

Now in Nazareth, less than a week later, just a few healings happen. Not only that, they appear to be simple ones that don't even deserve a mention. Perhaps headaches healed, muscle pain relieved, those kinds of healings. Nothing dramatic happened. Tragic. It was the same Jesus in both towns. Jesus carried the same anointing in both places. God's heart was to help the people in both towns. One town had faith, one town had doubt and unbelief.

WHO WAS TO BLAME FOR THE LACK OF FAITH?

Here are a couple other thoughts. It was the people at this "church" meeting that stopped what God wanted to do. It wasn't pagan Gentiles who didn't believe; it was Jews whose very history was full of miracles.

Who goes to church but the people who should have faith?
Who was the leader of the meeting? What did they say in the prelude to Jesus' sermon that quenched the anointing?
What songs did the worship band sing? Did they proclaim a great big God and cause hope to rise up? Or did they sing dirges and wonder where God was and when He was coming back?
What did husbands say to their wives and children as they walked to the meeting? Did they talk about their expectation or did they mutter about the routine of just another meeting, just another guest speaker? Did their kids ask, "Do we have to go?"

I guess you can see that I have been writing to myself in this chapter. I've been sharing where I have been and where I still am, to a certain degree. I am the culprit when nothing happens, not God.

JOHN WIMBER

I mentioned John Wimber earlier. He was a great man who profoundly affected the Christian church today. He helped to significantly change how we worship, the style of music, the lyrics of songs, etc. Before him we sang songs. Now we worship. John Wimber introduced body ministry back into churches. Church wasn't just about the man or woman of God who could preach, teach, minister, council, etc. I remember the first time John Wimber was at the revival in Toronto in June 1994. He sat on the stage for the whole of the ministry time and simply directed traffic.

John Wimber also believed in signs and wonders. Together with Peter C. Wagner, they reintroduced the concept that miracles were still possible. Pastors and theologians were shocked to hear that Fuller Seminary offered a class led by these two men.

There is the famous story of when John Wimber was born again. He had been a music producer, his most famous band being The Righteous Brothers. Remember "You've got that loving feeling"? John Wimber, then known as Johnny Wimber, brought that band together.

John took his wife, Carol, and their kids to church one Sunday after giving his life to Jesus. The meeting apparently was very boring for them. At the conclusion of the meeting, John Wimber talked to the pastor and asked him when the stuff would take place? The pastor was a bit confused and asked him to explain what he meant. Apparently John said something like, "When do we get to raise the dead and heal the sick like Jesus did?" The pastor told John those things didn't happen any more. To which John Wimber is credited with saying, "You mean I gave up rock and roll for this?"

Friends, have a big God. Don't ever put a limitation on what God can do. If you do, you and your unbelief are the problem, not God.

A man came to Jesus one day to ask for a miracle. Jesus asked him if he believed. His response needs to be ours: "*I do believe; help me overcome my unbelief*" (Mark 9:24). If you know that you are a doubter, begin to change that. Ask the Lord to cleanse you from lies, fears, and unbelief. He can and He will. If you are double-minded, decide to believe. Don't continue going back and forth. Make a decision that God is willing and able. And stick to it. James tells us that double-minded people get blown around and are useless (James 1:8). Put your feet down and take a stand.

Make a choice today to ask the Lord to give you new revelation regarding your life. Decide that you want to be led by the Spirit rather than by your soul. Value dreams and visions. This is the easy part. The tougher part is acting on what we know in our spirit. Take hope, your revelations from God, and put action steps to them. That takes us into the Faith Zone. Value taking risks.

Here are a couple prayers to reconnect to faith.

Father would you forgive me for all the times that I have shut you down. I acknowledge that you have wanted to do more in my life. My doubt and my unbelief have been the problem. Please forgive me. Please cleanse me from all the factors that influence me to not have faith. Come Holy Spirit and renew my mind so that I can know your wonderful plan and will for my life.

Father I am asking that you will grow my ability to believe. Help me to receive every thought that comes from you as a gift. Help me to act on what you reveal to me. Help me to live by faith and not based on facts, figures, test samples, etc. Father I want to live in the miraculous. I want

to see healings, signs, and wonders happen in my life. Mature me to
the place that I truly reflect your son Jesus, especially in the area of
obedience to your revelations. Amen.

GOING DEEPER

1. Ask Father God what factors from your past negatively affect your
   ability to believe for breakthroughs. Record his perspective on each
   of them. Make a choice to agree with the Lord.

2. Who do you blame for your past? Make a choice today to forgive them.
   How did you respond to that person? Picture them and the situation
   and say, "I chose to forgive you, honor you and release you in Jesus'
   name." Ask the Lord to forgive you for your negative reactions towards
   him or her. Ask God to clean you and break you free from your past.

ENDNOTES

[1] The Star of Bethlehem, bethlehemstar.com

[2] James or Jacob? Tradition says that when the first authorized translation of the Bible
into English was commissioned, King James wanted his name in the Bible. There
were no people named James. So the translators, who knew the desire of the king,
who knew he paid their salaries, and who perhaps knew what happened to people
who didn't obey the king, changed two of the Jacobs in the Bible to James. James
the brother of John, is a Jacob in the original Greek texts, as is James, the half-
brother of Jesus.

[3] James, the first pastor of the church in Jerusalem. James is the focal point for the
debate in Acts 15. When he speaks he makes the final decision. Several times Paul
comes to present his vision and mandate to James (Acts 21:18, Galatians 1:19).

[4] Bill and Gwen Prankard, bpea.com

CHAPTER 9

The Disciple with and Without Faith

MATTHEW 14

Shortly before dawn Jesus went out to them, walking on the lake. When the disciples saw him walking on the lake, they were terrified. "It's a ghost," they said, and cried out in fear. But Jesus immediately said to them: "Take courage. It is I. Don't be afraid." "Lord, if it's you," Peter replied, "tell me to come to you on the water." "Come," he said. Then Peter got down out of the boat, walked on the water and came toward Jesus. But when he saw the wind, he was afraid and, beginning to sink, cried out, "Lord, save me." Immediately Jesus reached out his hand and caught him. "You of little faith," he said, "why did you doubt?" And when they climbed into the boat, the wind died down. Then those who were in the boat worshiped him, saying, "Truly you are the Son of God." When they had crossed over, they landed at Gennesaret. And when the men of that place recognized Jesus, they sent word to all the surrounding country. People brought all their sick to him and begged him to let the sick just touch the edge of his cloak, and all who touched it were healed. MATTHEW 14:25-36

Recognition is such an important thing.

Israel has the Iron Dome. It is a computer program that is able to recognize the trajectory of a Hamas or Hezbola rocket and decide if it is a threat. If a threat, the computer launches an intercepting missile that knocks out the terrorist rocket. It computes this recognition calculation in seconds.

Most international airports have thermal recognition scans that are able to detect a person's body temperature. New arrivals go through the scan and are flagged if it appears they are carrying a virus such as H1N1 or SARS.

Facial recognition programs are everywhere. You don't have to be an enemy of the state like Jason Bourne to have governments scanning crowds for your face. The iPhoto program on my Apple computer is able to recognize people whom I have previously named. Is this Sandra Long? Yes? No?

THREE POSITIVE RECOGNITIONS

In this passage from Matthew 14 we see three different forms of recognition.

First, Peter recognized that it was Jesus and not a ghost that was walking on the water. Because of what he saw, he acted and walked on water. He got into the Faith Zone.

Second, when Peter recognized the effect that the wind was having on the waves, he acted in fear and almost drowned. Definitely not in the Faith Zone.

Third, when the good people of Gennesaret recognized Jesus, they brought all their sick friends and family, and an amazing healing meeting took place. Faith Zone stuff.

Peter is an amazing man. The Bible shows him at his best and worst. I believe the reason that so many of us identify more with Peter than the other disciples is his vulnerability. We see ourselves in him.

Peter (Simon) lived in Capernaum (Mark 1:21, 29). If archeologists are correct, he had one of the largest homes in the town. His home overlooked the Sea of Galilee. He had a corner home on the southwest side of the small town. Peter's home was expanded over time and made into a Christian church. Today there is a Catholic church built over his home.

We know that Peter owned fishing boats. He appears to have been in a partnership with his brother, Andrew, and another pair who were brothers, James and John, the sons of Zebedee (Mark 1:16–20). Andrew introduced Peter to Jesus. It was a dramatic encounter. Jesus immediately asked Peter to join him in ministry (John 1:41). Later, Jesus spoke identity and destiny into Peter's life and changed his name from pebbles (Simon) to rock (Peter) (Matthew 16:18).

Peter became the captain and spokesman of the Twelve. Not sure that they took a vote, or that he simply assumed the role. He was brash, not afraid to confront Jesus, and also not afraid to defend Jesus with a sword (John 18:10). Peter, perhaps more than any other of the Twelve, was in the process of having his life transformed as he travelled Galilee and Judea with Jesus.

A STORMY NIGHT

This story begins west of Capernaum. Jesus has just ministered to thousands of people. As we saw in chapter two, approximately 43,000 people have just had a free fish-on-a-bun meal. Not only that, but everyone who had sickness or pain has been healed. It was one of the seven meetings of Jesus where everyone was healed (Matthew 14:13–21).

> As evening approached, the disciples came to him and said, "This is a remote place, and it's already getting late. Send the crowds away, so they can go to the villages and buy themselves some food." MATTHEW 14:15

If it was evening before the feeding of these 43,000 people, you can imagine that it was well into the night before the crowds finally dispersed. As the crowd leaves, Jesus tells the Twelve to get into a boat and cross to the other side (Matthew 14:22). Jesus stays, dismisses the last of the crowd and then spends some time in prayer. During the prayer time he is aware that his men are struggling in a storm over the lake (Matthew 14:23).

Our story begins at dawn the next day. The sun is just about up. The night is almost over, but not the storm. The storm has lasted throughout the night. The men would have been exhausted physically and emotionally.

> Shortly before dawn Jesus went out to them, walking on the lake.
> MATTHEW 14:25

The narrative tells us something very interesting. Jesus wasn't walking to them, but beside them. The reason that Jesus is walking on the stormy seas is not to show off, but of necessity. He is caring for his team. Praying for them in this violent storm.

He saw the disciples straining at the oars, because the wind was against them. Shortly before dawn he went out to them, walking on the lake. He was about to pass by them. MARK 6:48

JESUS WAS PASSING BY

There are several stories of Jesus passing by people in the Gospels. It would appear that Jesus likes to be asked to help. His primary purpose wasn't to be a problem solver for all of life's issues. He wanted people to reach out for assistance. He wanted people to believe.

An example of this is the story of blind Bartimaeus (Mark 10:46–52). Jesus has just concluded a meeting in Jericho. The crowds are walking with him as he leaves the city. As Jesus is walking by, a blind beggar asks what all the fuss is about. Bartimaeus hears that it is Jesus. That is the good news. The bad news is that Jesus has passed him already. You will remember that he yells and screams trying to get Jesus' attention.

Finally, Jesus hears him. Bartimaeus throws off his beggar's overcoat (an amazing act of faith—he was confident that he wouldn't need it anymore) and is taken to Jesus. In a classic understated moment, Jesus asks the blind man what he wants. He wants to see. All Jesus does is say, *"Your faith has healed you"* (Mark 10:52).

Back to the Sea of Galilee, where Jesus is walking parallel to the boat.

The men are struggling in the midst of another infamous lake storm. Suddenly one of the men sees movement. He thinks he sees a man, or a ghost.

When the disciples saw him walking on the lake, they were terrified. "It's a ghost," they said, and cried out in fear. MATTHEW 14:26

FEAR IN A STORM AT NIGHT

Fear is a terrible thing. It robs people of their destiny. It destroys people's ability to make right choices. Fear cripples people from acting on what they know to be true. It kills people's dreams.

One of my extended family used to be afraid of spiders. This was not your average I-don't-like-them fear. This was panic fear. Twice she jumped out of a moving car because she thought she saw a spider. There was no spider, but the thought that there could be was enough to put her on the pavement. That is not good. Fear could kill you.

The disciples are freaking out. They see someone walking in the dim, predawn light. It can't be a person, as people can't walk on water. It must be a ghost. I am quite sure that the fear of a ghost nearby is now a bit more overwhelming than the storm. Their nerves have to be shattered.

But Jesus immediately said to them: "Take courage. It is I. Don't be afraid."
MATTHEW 14:27

Okay a ghost is one thing, but a talking ghost is even worse. This ghost is talking and he is looking right at them. However instead of saying "Boo," Jesus speaks hope and life to them. Jesus speaks right into their fears. Who is this person telling them not to be afraid? *"It is I"* isn't a great deal of help when you have no clue who it is you are talking to.

IS IT YOU?

I began this chapter with a list of recognition systems. Well, it would appear that Peter was the first one to come to the conclusion that if there is anyone capable of walking on water and offering hope, it is Jesus.

> *"Lord, if it's you," Peter replied, "tell me to come to you on the water."*
> MATTHEW 14:27

Now this is either one of the strongest faith statements ever uttered, or the stupidest. If this is a ghost, then you don't want to go near it. Undead spirits are constantly trying to trick people and kill them so they can have more undead friends. I've seen the movie trailers.

Peter's faith was exhibited in his assumption that this presence was Jesus. His action step was literally a step: walking out to Jesus. Peter has had a couple of these *"if it's you"* moments with Jesus. They were his light-bulb moments about Jesus, of what Jesus was capable of. Because of them, Peter was able to make the connection that this ghost was none other than Jesus.

Do you remember when Jesus asked to borrow Peter's boat to use as

a preaching station? Peter, knowing that the fish were not biting, responded to Jesus in the affirmative and they went out for *"a catch"* (Luke 5:4).
He will have another recognition moment after the resurrection of Jesus.
Peter will have an unsuccessful night fishing. Yet when a man, whom he
doesn't recognize, asks him to toss the net on the other side, he will do it.

It would appear that while Peter was a straight talker, a brash act-first-
think-later type, he did value revelation. He had a strong intuitive side. He
knew how God spoke to him.

Before we can move into the Faith Zone, where breakthroughs and miracles happen, we must first learn that when God speaks, He isn't always
obvious and clear. God wants us to learn to hear and sense His still quiet
nudges. Yes, He often speaks boldly and loudly, but more frequently it is
with a whisper.

Peter has one of those moments again. Could this be Jesus? If it is Jesus,
it is safer to be with him on the water than in the boat in a storm. Good
point Peter. He asks the question. *"Lord, if it's you," Peter replied, "tell me to
come to you on the water"* (Matthew 14:27).

COME

The ghost says one word. *"'Come,' he said. Then Peter got down out of the
boat, walked on the water and came toward Jesus"* (Matthew 14:29).

Wow. As far as I know, walking on water is still not a normal occurrence.
Peter does what no one other than Jesus has ever done. In fact, Peter is

starting at a disadvantage. Jesus would have started in shallow water, by the shore. Peter is starting in the middle of the lake in a storm with large waves. Those are bragging points later on. I am not sure what was happening in the boat at this moment. His brother Andrew may have been trying to talk sense into him. Thomas, I am sure was freaking out. No one else was confident that this ghost was actually Jesus. No one else wanted to take the risk.

Peter steps over the side of the railing. The side of the boat would be about 3 feet high (1 meter). Over he goes. I'm quite confident that Peter does this with gusto rather than caution.

Peter was going to find out right away whether this is Jesus or a ghost. Turns out he was in the Faith Zone. Because he was confident it was Jesus who said, "Come," Peter acted. Because Peter acted on the revelation, he entered the area of the miraculous. Physics and natural law have no authority in this zone. Father God lives in this realm. Peter walked on the water. A miracle. He did something that many have attempted but none have achieved.

At each of our tours in Israel we spend a couple days by the Sea of Galilee. Usually we take some time by the beach where Jesus fed the 5,000. We take off our shoes and wade into the water. Someone always says, "Let's walk on the water." We all try, but it doesn't happen. Why? While we know it is possible, we don't believe it is possible. Deep down our minds have convinced us that it isn't going to happen.

We don't know how many steps Peter took on the water. My guess is ten or more bold faith steps. The passage clearly says that he was *walking* on the water.

Then Peter got down out of the boat, walked on the water and came toward Jesus. MATTHEW 14:29

FEAR VERSES FAITH

I've said this many times already, but here it is again. The enemy of faith is fear. Doubt comes when we begin to listen to Satan. Satan is a lawyer and he reminds us of the facts. Doubt escalates to fear once we believe whatever lie he is peddling this time. Satan is always challenging what the Lord says to us. Adam and Eve experienced this in the garden: "Did God say..." Jesus experienced it in the desert: "If you are the son of God...."

Nagging thoughts attack the rhema word of the Lord. Our confidence in what we heard hangs in the balance at this moment. Do we say, "Behind me Satan," or do we go quiet like Adam did as Eve was being misled? Adam's doubt in the truth about eating the fruit leads to the first sin. The Bible is very clear that Adam stood silent beside Eve as she was tempted (Genesis 3:1–6). He knew what God had spoken, yet doubt froze him into doing nothing to defend and cover his wife. His sin was the first, not Eve's.

When God talks and we act, the Scriptures call that faith. When Satan talks and we act, we call that fear. The choice of which voice to obey is ours.

Peter was amazing. He walked on water. I'm sure he also heard voices challenging him. I want you to understand how fast we flip from revelation to fear. We go from walking to sinking without notice. It can be instantaneous.

But when he saw the wind, he was afraid and, beginning to sink, cried out,
"Lord, save me." MATTHEW 14:30

WHAT DO WE SEE?

The Faith Zone is not dependent on what we know in our heads, the facts
we have at hand, or what we have figured out. Faith is not a natural sight
issue. It is a knowing something in your spirit. When Peter saw the wind,
fear struck. Peter allowed himself to be distracted. Instead of looking at
Jesus, his gaze turned to a large wave the storm was bringing his way. He
sank. The obvious lesson here is we need to train our eyes to stay focused
on Jesus. Watching horror movies is clearly going to take our focus off
what is holy and righteous, and lead us into fear. Viewing porn on the
Internet is clearly not an act that will help us focus on Jesus.

Jesus said quite a bit about our eyes. We need to train our eyes or get rid
of them (Matthew 5:29). I don't think that Jesus actually expected us to
gouge our eyes out. I believe he was using a metaphor to encourage us to
learn what is acceptable to look at. One of the most profound verses of
the Bible is hidden away in the book of Job. Job says, *"I made a covenant
with my eyes not to look lustfully at a young woman"* (Job 31:1). Wow. As a
husband and father, Job knows that one of his battles is looking at young
women and entering into fantasy. He has learned to bounce his eyes off
ladies and not take a second look.

Sidebar about seeing. One of the best books that many need to read is
Every Man's Battle.[1] This great book teaches men some very practical ways

to keep from entering into sexual fantasy and to cleanse themselves once they've crossed the line.

Back to Peter. *"But when he saw the wind, he was afraid and, beginning to sink, cried out, 'Lord, save me'"* (Matthew 14:30). Did you see the word *"sink"*? The Greek word is *katapontizesthai*. It literally means to plunge under the water and drown. Peter was fully under the surface of the water. He was not simply falling into the waves, he was under the surface and dropping fast. His life was in peril.

What happened to the Faith Zone? It vanished. Looking at one wave, listening to the howling wind, and believing one lie of Satan had disastrous results. Peter was about to drown.

PETER'S RESCUE

What happens next was probably another miracle. Jesus rescued Peter dramatically. *"Immediately Jesus reached out his hand and caught him"* (Matthew 14:31). Peter, sinking below the water line, shouts out with water gurgling in his mouth, *"Lord, save me."*

Is this prayer, *"Lord, save me,"* a command or a request? Peter knew that Jesus could save him and so he spoke it out. He moved back into the Faith Zone. His action was to cry for help and to reach out his hand. I can't prove that Peter reached out his hand, but we know that Jesus grabbed on to something.

Let me share another interesting word with you. The Greek word for *"reached out his hand"* gives a picture about Jesus that you may not have thought about. The Greek isn't reached out, rather, out reached. Is it possible that while Peter was sinking below the water, Jesus' arm lengthened? If Jesus was standing and Peter was under the water, we are talking about a big gap. Peter was potentially several feet below the surface already.

If I'm right, Peter was clearly in the Faith Zone again. His prayer was not a hopeful request, rather a command that brought a miracle his way. If my theory on this is accurate, Peter moved from faith to fear and back to faith all within a few seconds. That's good news for you and me. We can get back into the Faith Zone as soon as we realize that doubts have taken us out.

Peter was a disciple with faith. He was also the disciple with little faith. Look at what Jesus said to him: *"Immediately Jesus reached out his hand and caught him. 'You of little faith,' he said, 'why did you doubt?'"* (Matthew 14:31). This conversation took place as they walked on the water back to the boat. I can imagine that Jesus had his hand around Peter in a loving grasp, as well as one that was holding him up.

Jesus addressed the issue right away. It's doubt. Doubt is the opposite of hope. Fear is the opposite of faith. Hope inspires us to action. Doubt also inspires us to action as well, but with very negative results.

LITTLE FAITH

Jesus uses the word *little* to describe Peter's revelation. He was not saying

Peter had no faith, but that his understanding of what God could do was still small. He was at the beginner stage. Friends this is amazing news for us. If little faith allows you to walk on the water, what does great faith or even above-average faith get us?

I'm sure most of you have seen plaques with the "Footprints" poem. The question to Jesus in the poem is about his presence when there were only one set of footprints. The punch line is that those were hard times, and Jesus was carrying us. Peter had one of these experiences. Sometimes God leads us gently but other times we go through the fire and through the waters. I want to remind you what God says though. He has a confidence in His ability to get us to the places He wants us to be.

The reaction of the men in the boat to Peter and Jesus walking back has to be compelling. I definitely want to see the footage of this when I get to heaven. Do you think there were high fives, or silence? I'm leaning towards the stunned silence.

And when they climbed into the boat, the wind died down. Then those who were in the boat worshiped him, saying, "Truly you are the Son of God."
MATTHEW 14:32-33

Instantly the storm ends. The eleven other guys go into glory mode. They begin to worship Jesus in tongues. Yiddish, Greek, and Aramaic. How do you put into words what you have just seen? You can't. You are simply left to worship in awe.

MIRACLES IN NIGERIA

Many years ago I was invited to accompany John and Carol Arnott to see T.B. Joshua in Nigeria. I know there is some controversy surrounding him. He is a very unique man with great anointing, in my opinion. In the same way that critics of the Toronto Blessing have diminished over time, so the criticism of Prophet Joshua has let up. He has outlasted most of his adversaries and lots of good fruit has lasted.

I remember a moment at T.B. Joshua's church when I was one of the guys in the boat trying to figure out what just happened. It led me to blubber like a baby, to repent for my very limited faith, and to worship the Lord. As all guests are when visiting The Synagogue: Church of All Nations,[2] we were chaperoned by members of their staff. Our group, folks from Catch The Fire Toronto and personal friends of John and Carol, got to have a behind-the-scenes experience.

At our first healing meeting on the Wednesday we were awakened early in the morning. We saw a stampede of people rushing through the gates to queue for the approximately one thousand chairs set up for those needing healing. Each person had to have a doctor's certificate. They also had a personal interview on camera where they said who they were, where they came from, and what their physical need was. I too went through this process when I asked for prayer for my eyes.

After watching the near riot for these seats, we had breakfast. Then it was back down to the auditorium area to observe the interviews, and to be taken to the severe cases. We saw the section where those with AIDS and HIV would sit. We saw the area for those battling cancer. We also saw a row of cars in a street beside the church complex. Inside each car were people who were too weak or too handicapped to come into the building.

Often a bench was placed outside of the car for them and their family to sit. On one of these benches we saw a lady whose joints were completely atrophied. Her fingers, wrists, knees, ankles, and toes were all gnarled. Her fingers were bent back completely to her wrist. There was no wriggle room; they were stiff. She had two sons with her. They were holding the large sign that recorded her name, where she was from, and what her problem was.

The meeting began about ten in the morning. Choirs sang, pastors gave brief sermons, videos testimonies of people who had been previously healed where shown. People would come and go for snacks and water as the meeting went on. That service lasted more than eight hours. About three in the afternoon pastor Joshua appeared. He came to the guest area where we were seated on white plastic garden chairs. He greeted us as well as the royal Nigerians who were all dressed in spectacular outfits. These distinguished people were local mayors and village kings and queens who are a part of the congregation.

Prophet Joshua took the microphone, shared stories, and gave a short twenty-minute sermon. All the Western guests, about 25 of us, were then invited to follow him for the next three hours as he ministered to the sick.

He walked outside to the cars. He went to the lady whom we had met earlier that day. He looked at her and did nothing. My recollection is that he pondered for about 30 seconds and then walked to the next car. This got a huge reaction from the two sons. They screamed and cried out for the Prophet to do something. He didn't. He moved on to the next car and healed that person as the shouting continued just a car length away.

I don't even remember what was wrong with the person in the second car. I'm not the most compassionate person, but I was drawn to the seeming harshness of this "man of God" who did nothing. Why?

T.B. did return to the lady after healing those in other cars. The sons continued to plead for their mother as she sat on this wooden bench, unable to move. Every joint was stiff and disfigured. T.B. stood again in front of this lady and looked at her. He had a handheld microphone and tapped it to make sure it was working. Several camera crews followed him. Those inside the sanctuary got to see what was going on outside courtesy of these technical teams and hundreds of TV screens.

My favourite part was the play-by-play team who provided ongoing commentary to fill in the gaps. The pair were the cheerleaders for the church, they explained what the pastor was doing, how he was doing it, etc. They sat inside the auditorium watching everything from monitors, just like at a sporting event. T.B. Joshua then casually tapped the lady on all of her joints. He touched her shoulders, elbows, wrists, hips, knees and ankles. I remember him saying one phrase, "I command you to stand up." She stood.

He tapped the same joints again. He said, "I command you to walk." Within seconds the stiffness in her joints was gone. Her fingers were normal, her toes were normal, everything was normal. Perhaps three seconds later she was running. Totally healed. I was in shock. I began to sob. The smallness of my faith had been exposed by that miracle. I remember an overwhelming feeling that I wasn't even born again. I knew I was, but the simplicity of the healing was revealing so much immaturity in the way I knew God.

That is what happened in the boat as Jesus and Peter walked back. Shock, disbelief, and fear all gave way to worship. Everything changed because of this miracle. The sun came out and the sky turned blue. The rest of the trip to Gennesaret was very different.

FAITH IN GENNESARET

The last couple verses in this passage are very interesting to me. Look at how the people of Gennesaret respond to Jesus. Look at their faith levels; a sharp contrast to the men in the boat.

> When they had crossed over, they landed at Gennesaret. And when the men of that place recognized Jesus, they sent word to all the surrounding country. People brought all their sick to him and begged him to let the sick just touch the edge of his cloak, and all who touched it were healed. MATTHEW 14:34-36

What revelation do these people have? They knew that Jesus could heal. Their action was to bring their sick friends and family members to Jesus. They begged Jesus to let them touch the edge of his garments. All who did were healed. These folks quickly entered the Faith Zone.

Capernaum was only a few miles away. I'm guessing that the people of Gennesaret heard the story of the lady who was healed by touching the bottom of Jesus' cloak. They believed that if it happened once, it could happen again. If twelve years of bleeding can be healed by a touch, why can't their sickness?

I love the word *all*. Everyone who believed that a touch was good enough got their healing. God rewards faith. Faith puts a smile on His face. The passage says, *"all who touched it were healed."* This gives me the impression that not everyone touched his garment. Those who didn't have faith didn't get the reward.

Guess who was also at this meeting? The Twelve were there. Peter and his buddies got another chance to see how simple it is to enter the Faith Zone. I'm sure the experience from the Sea of Galilee, combined with an "all" healing meeting, helped them to increase their faith. Did Matthew, remembering this event, purposely link these two stories together? Did he connect Jesus reaching out to Peter with the people reaching out and touching Jesus?

The people of Gennesaret would be the lower income people in Israel. They were on the wrong side of the Sea of Galilee. This is the Golan Heights area of Israel today. The area has lots of hills. It isn't the best agricultural land, and it's desolate.

EVERYONE CAN HAVE FAITH

Their humble circumstances did not stop these people from acting on revelation though. All of us have the same opportunities to believe. Faith isn't for the rich or the poor. It isn't for one particular cultural group or any one gender. One of Paul's early revelations was this: *"There is neither Jew nor Gentile, neither slave nor free, nor is there male and female, for you are all one in Christ Jesus"* (Galatians 3:28). Everyone has an equal standing and opportunity because of Jesus.

Peter had the same revelation the day God showed him the blanket of unclean animals. *"Then Peter began to speak: 'I now realize how true it is that God does not show favoritism but accepts from every nation the one who fears him and does what is right'"* (Acts 10:34-35). Because God reveals himself to each of us, because we all have the ability to connect with what God communicates, we can all receive hope. When God stirs up hope in our spirit, we all have the option to act or to sit still. If we do what our Father says we move into this unique place we're calling the Faith Zone.

Peter stepped in, then out, then back in. This is how life is. We believe, we doubt, we believe again. My hope for you is that you will be inspired by what I am sharing. That you will see how easy it is to access the supernatural kingdom simply by believing, by acting on revelation.

Father, help us never to get discouraged because we doubt. Instead give us a second chance just like Peter had. Allow us to have opportunity after opportunity to connect to you. Help us to be like the people of Gennesaret and reach out to touch you. Amen.

GOING DEEPER

1. I'd like you to remember a dark night in your past. Perhaps the death of a loved one, a health issue, or a financial struggle. Ask the Lord to remind you of three negative emotions you had. Jot them down.

2. Psalm 23 tells us that Jesus our shepherd is with us in the valley of the shadow of death. Ask him to show you where he was during this dark time from your past. Talk to him about these three emotions. What do you need to know? Record what he speaks.

3. Psalm 23 tells us that during these times of darkness Jesus, our shepherd, anoints us with oil. Ask the Lord what special gift God gave you at that time? Record these gifts. Print them out. Post them where you can see them daily and thank God for these gifts.

ENDNOTES

[1]Stephen Arterburn and Fred Stoeker, *Every Man's Battle: Winning the War on Sexual Temptation One Victory at a Time* (WaterBrook Press, 2004).

[2]The Synagogue: Church of All Nations, www.scoan.org

CHAPTER 10

The Woman with Great Faith

MATTHEW 15

Leaving that place, Jesus withdrew to the region of Tyre and Sidon. A Canaanite woman from that vicinity came to him, crying out, "Lord, Son of David, have mercy on me. My daughter is demon-possessed and suffering terribly." Jesus did not answer a word. So his disciples came to him and urged him, "Send her away, for she keeps crying out after us." He answered, "I was sent only to the lost sheep of Israel." The woman came and knelt before him. "Lord, help me." she said. He replied, "It is not right to take the children's bread and toss it to the dogs." "Yes it is, Lord," she said. "Even the dogs eat the crumbs that fall from their master's table." Then Jesus said to her, "Woman, you have great faith. Your request is granted." And her daughter was healed at that moment. MATTHEW 15:21–28

I have a confession. During my high-school years, I was a bit of a prankster. A couple friends and I did some relatively harmless things to get a laugh. That's our opinion of harmless. One Halloween we set a pumpkin on fire outside the home of one of our teachers. It was just a small explosion. Let's say there was lots of pumpkin on his lawn. He was nice to us the next day in class. I suspect that he knew it was my group of friends.

Our high school had a grassy knoll that served as the bleachers for sporting events. The track and football field were between the knoll and the school. We once set a delayed fuse to a small area of dead grass on the hill where the pot smokers would sit. It went off about five minutes after we left the area. While they were busily trying to put out the fire, the teachers came and caught them smoking.

Our principal would give short speeches at our assemblies. As he talked we arranged for the curtains behind him to be opened. It revealed his car on the stage. He was not happy and the assembly was cut short that day. How we got his keys is a secret for another book.

Perhaps the most labour-intensive prank we pulled related to steeplechase hurdles. You may have seen Olympic track and field events where one of the races has very high hurdles that span the width of the track. There is also a water pit at the base of one of the hurdles. Well the night before our school hosted our regional track and field event, several of us made up our own obstacle course. We hoisted the hurdles onto the roof of our high school and set the event up there. School officials had no idea where the hurdles where until they looked up. Sadly, one of them broke as the officials tried to get them down from the roof. Of course we were there to watch and soak in the glory of our prank!

As an adult, I've learnt to move hurdles of a different kind. Many people don't like hurdles and other obstacles. We are frustrated by them and view them as delays. God, however, seems to like them. A very interesting thing happens on the way into the Faith Zone. Speed bumps show up. Blockades appear. Obstacles arrive to stop us from living in faith.

These hurdles test if we really believe the revelation that God has given us. Hurdles are a part of the faith journey. We have to learn to jump over these obstructions or move them out of the way. In Matthew 15 we read the story of a second person that Jesus says has great faith. The first, you will remember, was the Roman centurion from Capernaum. We looked at his story in chapter three.

Jesus designates only two people as having great faith: one a man, one a woman. Both Gentiles. One is from Rome, the other from modern-day Lebanon. In both stories the person who received the breakthrough wasn't the one asking for it. Neither of the beneficiaries of the great faith were a part of the conversations or even there to meet Jesus.

Let's look at the story.

> A Canaanite woman from that vicinity came to him, crying out, "Lord, Son of David, have mercy on me. My daughter is demon-possessed and suffering terribly." MATTHEW 15:22

Every single time that someone came to Jesus with a request, he granted it. When the leper asked if Jesus was willing to heal him, he was (Matthew 8:1-3). When Mary, his mother, asked him to do something about the lack of wine at the wedding in Cana, he did (John 2:5-8).

Another sidebar for you, this one about timetables. Bill Johnson talks about being able to receive the benefits that we know are ours but happen to be out of season.[1] He gives two examples of this. The first is this wedding where Mary confronts her son. Jesus tells his mom that his start time for miracles is still a bit away.

"Nonsense" Mary says, "I know that you are supposed to be doing miracles, get started" (my paraphrase of John 2:5). Mary accesses something before God's set time.

The second example is this Canaanite lady. She too is going to receive rewards designated for years later. Jesus is not yet ministering to Gentiles. This small detail isn't going to slow her down. Her revelation will bring the future forward. The problem is her daughter. Her girl is *"demon-possessed and suffering terribly."* In my reading of the gospel accounts of Jesus, about one-third of all of the healing stories involve demonic spirits.

In Luke's account, there are eighteen healing stories and in half of them spirits are mentioned as contributors to the sickness or disease. This is both good news and bad. The good is that when we discern the spirit and how it got there, we can easily get it out from the person. The bad is that people often freak out and take offence when someone suggests that perhaps this is a spirit of affliction, rather than arthritis.

For some reason Western believers have difficulty acknowledging that spirits have the power to negatively affect them. Somehow we see this as an attack on our self-esteem. We often refuse the spiritual diagnosis and the helpful prayer that would follow. Most other nations of the world don't have this problem. They are very comfortable with the reality of active demons and angels. They humble themselves, receive ministry, and find freedom.

This Canaanite lady knows the root issue in her daughter is a demon, not a disease. She doesn't hide this reality. Luke 13:11 relates the story of when Jesus met a lady that everyone else thought had osteoporosis. Her back had been curved for eighteen years. The doctors of the day were not able to do anything for her. But Jesus, when he discerns that it is the spirit of affliction, frees her with a word. This lady from Tyre wants that kind of ministry from Jesus on behalf of her daughter. This is where the obstacles kick in. There are three hurdles she needs to overcome.

The first hurdle is silence, the second relates to timing, and the third is about her culture.

HURDLE #1: SILENCE

Jesus did not answer a word. So his disciples came to him and urged him, "Send her away, for she keeps crying out after us." He answered, "I was sent only to the lost sheep of Israel." The woman came and knelt before him. "Lord, help me." she said. MATTHEW 15:23-25

Jesus is silent. He doesn't respond to her.

Friends this happens all the time. We know something or we think we have a revelation and then silence. Nothing happens. Do we give up or do we push in? This lady pushes in. She keeps *"crying out"* to Jesus. She bothers the disciples so much that they ask Jesus to do something. What they want is for Jesus to *"send her away."* I love the lack of compassion of the disciples. They reflect our selfish hearts way too often don't they?

When there is silence in heaven, please don't give up. Keep pushing in. Keep praying. Keep asking the Lord for further clarification and more insights. Crying out provokes a reaction from Jesus. After perhaps a few minutes of silence, Jesus finally speaks. He tells her why he was silent. *"He answered, 'I was sent only to the lost sheep of Israel'"* (Matthew 15:24).

HURDLE #2: TIMING

The second obstacle Jesus raises is timing. He isn't doing miracles for Gentiles yet. His ministry is only to Jews. Others, such as Peter and Paul, will initiate the next phase. There will be a time when Gentiles are able to connect with the benefits of the kingdom, but not now. While we don't know the timeline from this lady to Cornelius (Acts 10), we do know that the Gentiles don't experience salvation until several years later.

Matthew doesn't tell us the exact revelation that this lady has, but whatever it is, this timeline nonsense from Jesus doesn't stop her either. She pushes in further and humbles herself even more. Instead of simply shouting her request, she approaches Jesus on her knees. *"The woman came and knelt before him. 'Lord, help me,' she said"* (Matthew 15:25).

The symbolism here is of persistent prayer. You and I are encouraged to pray without ceasing (1 Thessalonians 5:17). That is exactly what she did.

HURDLE #3: REJECTION

The third obstacle is a cultural one. Jesus uses a racial slur towards Gentiles and refers to this lady and her daughter as a dogs. *He replied, "It is not right to take the children's bread and toss it to the dogs"* (Matthew 15:22). It sounds a bit harsh, doesn't it? I think this was a purposeful bump in the road to see if the mother would abandon her pursuit of freedom for her daughter. She doesn't waver in the least. She is going to step around this obstacle as well.

I used to struggle with Jesus' response to this lady until I personally met Orthodox Jews. Let me explain.

Sandra and I love going to Israel and we have a love for the Jewish people. I personally feel that it is the responsibility of every follower of Jesus to pray for the peace of Jerusalem. Not only that, but to support Israel as much as we can. When I say that I am a supporter of Israel I am not saying that the government doesn't do things wrong or that other faith groups are automatically second-class citizens. What I am saying is that if God is on Israel's side, so am I.

Orthodox Jews are a very peculiar people group. They earnestly seek to live by the letter of the Old Testament law. They separate themselves from anything that would make them unclean, including Gentiles.

TREATED LIKE DOGS

On our first flight to Israel many years ago, we saw the implications of what it means for the Orthodox Jews to honour their version of Old Testament teachings. None of the men would sit beside a Gentile woman on the airplane. A Gentile man is okay, but not the ladies. The reason is that this unknown woman may be in the middle of her period. If they were to inadvertently touch, he would be unclean. God bless the British Airways flight attendants, but they had the laborious task of rearranging the seating arrangements.

Then, just before the flight was to take off, the Orthodox men got out of their seats on mass. They put down mats in the bulkhead areas, knelt, and said their prayers facing Jerusalem. No flight attendant was able to convince them that it was unsafe to be doing this while we were taxiing to the runway.

Sandra and I happened to have one of those bulkhead seats. As soon as the fasten seat belt signs was turned off when we were in the air, the men gathered in front of our seats again. As more of them joined the group, they began to invade our space. They ignored us and treated us like (can I say it?) dogs. We understood exactly what was going on and tried not take any offence. They were simply doing what they had been taught to do. The men gathered to talk and discuss while the women stayed in their seats and looked after the children.

At one point Sandra did get fed up. They were stepping on her toes. They were pushing in to her. They didn't acknowledge that they were in our space. Sandra needed to use the toilet. She stood up, placed her hands on the men closest to her, parted them, and walked to the lavatory. Oops, now a couple of men had to purify themselves. Sandra did feel better though.

Gentiles knew this was how the Jews saw them in that day. They understood it was how things were, whether they liked it or not. Apparently this Gentile lady was not put off by Jesus' use of the word *dog*. She used it to her own advantage.

> *"Yes it is, Lord," she said. "Even the dogs eat the crumbs that fall from their master's table."* MATTHEW 15:27

That statement is enough for her to enter the Faith Zone. This is what Jesus responds to. He hears this amazing statement of faith. He agrees with her and the daughter is healed from a distance. I love it.

> *Then Jesus said to her, "Woman, you have great faith. Your request is granted." And her daughter was healed at that moment.* MATTHEW 15:28

As I've stated earlier in the chapter, this woman was the second person to reach into heaven and get her breakthrough prematurely. First was Mary, the mother of Jesus, and now this lady.

When there was silence from heaven, she pushed in.
When there was a delay because of timing, she prayed more.
When there was a possible insult, she turned it into her miracle.

Obstacles frequently arise. They help to define us. They make us better people, more God-conscious people. They pave the way for great miracles.

The premise for my book on the life of David (*On The Run*) is that David simply wasn't ready to become the next king of Israel. He hadn't learned to overcome obstacles. His heart wasn't yet tuned to God's to the point that he could step into the prophetic word that stated he would be a man after God's heart. If David hadn't had three years on the run, hiding from King Saul, he would have been a poor replacement. Obstacles defined David. They made him a more sensitive leader with a heart after God.

WHO BRINGS OBSTACLES?

One thing we need to sort out: Does God bring the obstacles or does the devil?

To be honest, I don't know that I can give a definitive answer to this. This answer is slightly above my pay grade. What I do know is that either way—if we hold on, take our stand, and push in—God gets the glory and we get our breakthroughs.

The reward for not giving in when the enemy tempts us is that God provides a way out for us (1 Corinthians 10:13). If Jesus' experience in the wilderness is also true for us, then just as angels ministered to Jesus, we can expect unseen angels beginning to help us mature in the anointing (Matthew 4:11). That is a great reward for resisting temptations.

When difficult times and trials come, God redeems them for our benefit. Somehow, our value and worth to the kingdom goes up. The problem with success is that we don't know what we did right. The benefit of failure is we know exactly what not to do the next time.

In this you greatly rejoice, though now for a little while you may have had
to suffer grief in all kinds of trials. These have come so that your faith, of
greater worth than gold, which perishes even though refined by fire, may be
proved genuine and may result in praise, glory and honour when Jesus Christ
is revealed. 1 PETER 1:6-7

When the church was persecuted in Acts 8:1 and everyone was running for their lives, God turned it around and expanded the church. Ordinary people stepped up and brought revival to the places where they settled.

Philip stepped into the Faith Zone and brought great joy to a Samaritan city. Great miracles and deliverances happened because of persecution (Acts 8:4-8). The most famous man in town came to know the Lord. Philip persevered.

Several other unnamed men also escaped the persecution in Jerusalem. They went to Antioch and founded one of the largest churches of that time. Eventually, Barnabas and Paul would take over leadership of that dynamic apostolic church (Acts 11:19-30).

James 1:2-4 tells us that trials make us better people. We need to make the choice to grow when difficult times come, instead of becoming bitter. Each time hurdles come up we need to be pushing into God for more revelation, praying more fervently, and not taking offence at God or others.

I'd like to take us back to chapter one. We began by looking at Hebrews 11 and observing the ancients, people who lived this faith thing centuries ago.

I'd like to remind you of some of the obstacles these folks encountered and what they accomplished.

ABEL

By acting on revelation Abel brought God a better offering than Cain did. By acting on revelation he was commended as righteous, when God spoke well of his offerings. And by acting on revelation Abel still speaks, even though he is dead. HEBREWS 11:4

Cain failed the obedience test; Able passed it. Abel gave his offering immediately, while Cain gave his *"in the course of time"* (Genesis 4:3). Both heard God speak; one brother acted right away, one brother didn't. Abel was rewarded, Cain got bitter.

NOAH

By acting on revelation Noah, when warned about things not yet seen, in holy fear built an ark to save his family. By his acting on revelation he condemned the world and became heir of the righteousness that is in keeping with acting on revelation. HEBREWS 11:7

Noah passed the time and the compromise tests. It took him 120 years to build the ark. He also lived with the wickedest generation that had ever lived. Noah kept on fearing God.

SARAH

And by acting on revelation even Sarah, who was past childbearing age, was enabled to bear children because she considered him faithful who had made the promise. And so from this one man, and he as good as dead, came descendants as numerous as the stars in the sky and as countless as the sand on the seashore. HEBREWS 11:11–12

One night Sarah asked Abraham to come to bed (aka, "Let's have sex tonight"). There were two huge obstacles blocking that statement of faith. First, Sarah was *past childbearing age*. Second, Abraham's body was *as good as dead*. Viagra was invented for men whose body parts don't work. Sorry to be that graphic, but that is what this passage is about.

Sarah remembered what the two angels had prophesied to her and Abraham. Despite two great obstacles to produce a child, she initiated for them to try once more. Sarah entered the Faith Zone. Good news friends: having sex with your spouse can be an act of faith.

ABRAHAM

By acting on revelation Abraham, when God tested him, offered Isaac as a sacrifice. He who had embraced the promises was about to sacrifice his one and only son, even though God had said to him, "It is through Isaac that your offspring will be reckoned." Abraham reasoned that God could even raise the dead, and so in a manner of speaking he did receive Isaac back from death.
HEBREWS 11:17–19

When God asked Abraham to kill his promised son, *"Abraham reasoned that God could even raise the dead"*. Had people ever been raised from the dead? NO. Abraham must have thought, *The impossible has to become possible if God wants me to kill my son. He is my promise.* You know the rest, how the Lord provided a ram and Abraham's son was spared.

JOSHUA

By acting on revelation the walls of Jericho fell, after the army had marched around them for seven days. **HEBREWS 11:30**

When Joshua presented his battle plan to take down Jericho by walking around the city, no one questioned him. Why? They believed him when he said that he had met with the angel of the armies of the Lord (Joshua 5). All the people of Israel actively entered into faith for something that physics said was impossible. By marching in accordance with a revelation given to their leader, city walls fell down.

FAITHFUL ONES

Women received back their dead, raised to life again. There were others who were tortured, refusing to be released so that they might gain an even better resurrection. Some faced jeers and flogging, and even chains and imprisonment. They were put to death by stoning; they were sawed in two; they were killed by the sword. They went about in sheepskins and goatskins, destitute, persecuted and mistreated—the world was not worthy of them.

They wandered in deserts and mountains, living in caves and in holes in the
ground. HEBREWS 11:35-38

Look at the list of obstacles that people faced. Normal people may give up, but not them. They knew something. They had revelation from the Lord.

Death didn't stop them from believing.
Torture didn't stop them from hoping.
Persecution didn't stop them from looking ahead.

Remember that faith is hearing, acting, and then receiving the rewards. When we act on the revelation we have from the Lord, we move into the Faith Zone where everything and anything is possible.

WHAT WAS THEIR REWARD?

These were all commended for their acting on revelation, yet none of them
received what had been promised, since God had planned something
better for us so that only together with us would they be made perfect.
HEBREWS 11:39-40

These people never gave up on what they felt God said. They never surrendered their dreams to the circumstances and popular culture. What about the Canaanite woman who didn't let rejection get in her way? Obstacles rendered her reward all the better.

Then Jesus said to her, "Woman, you have great faith. Your request is granted."
And her daughter was healed at that moment. MATTHEW 15:28

Her daughter was instantly cleansed from the evil assignment on her life. She was free from all the demonic pain. This happened because of her mom's faith.

This lady had two simple revelations that caused hope to rise up in her heart. She verbalized her hope and was rewarded by a great healing/deliverance. I believe her first revelation was that despite the fact that Jesus wasn't yet healing Gentiles, sooner or later it was going to happen.

Can I suggest that the story of the wedding in Cana, about 20 miles (32 km) away, may have influenced her boldness? Did she know that Mary, the mother of Jesus, had changed the timing of Jesus' first miracle? Had she heard that a mother had changed God's plans? Could she also do this? If so, why not here? Why not now?

What if she didn't know the story of Mary? Then her statements to Jesus are all the more powerful. A Gentile woman knew that sozo (the Greek word for salvation, deliverance, and healing) started with the Jews but would eventually come her way.

Second, she knew that all she needed was the faith of a mustard seed. She simply asked for a "crumb." This is great news for us. She didn't need Jesus to come to her home. She didn't need hands laid on her daughter. She didn't need a long prayer. She just needed a crumb. Wow.

WE HAVE MORE REVELATION

Friends, you and I have more revelation today than this mother did. We should know God's heart better now than any other generation.

First, we have the whole Bible. This lady was still relying on revelation from the Old Testament. She didn't have the full story. Despite that, she was able to reach into the future and get what she needed.

Second, the Bible says that the kingdom of God is always advancing. God is always working and more is getting done (John 5:17). This means that breakthroughs and miracles are getting easier. Gloria a Dios.

Most of us have heard a story of someone who knows someone who was raised from the dead. That is because we have history on our side. Resurrections are happening more often. Most of us know of people who were diagnosed with an incurable disease and are still living, free from that label. That is because the kingdom is advancing each day. Most of us know someone who had no money and God came through with a financial miracle. That is because more is possible today. Most of us know someone who didn't find their spouse until their fifties, and they are absolutely enjoying their marriage. That is because of eHarmony. Just kidding.

We know the stories, yes? We have even lived the stories, yes? So are we going to let a few hurdles get in our way this time? Are we going to give up when our miracle is right around the corner?

I love the story in John 21 where some of the disciples fished all night without any success. The 153 fish that they caught after Jesus showed up were simply a boat-width away the whole time. God had assembled all those large fish, but they were swimming on the other side of the boat. They were just waiting for the disciples to respond to a word from Jesus and try the other side. Awesome.

Folks, faith is not supposed to be hard. Hear from the Lord, value what He says, then act on it. This puts us in the zone. Faith is acting on revelation.

Father, thank you for the amazing stories in our Bible. We know that they are there to inspire us and teach us how to live by faith. Father, help us to not get tripped up by obstacles. May we endure, persevere, and overcome. We pray this in Jesus' name, amen.

GOING DEEPER

1. When there is silence from heaven, how do you normally react?

2. When God tells you "not now" or "wait," how do you respond?

3. When you feel rejected, perhaps even by Father God, what do you do?

4. Record your answers to the above questions, and then ask, "Lord, what do you want to say to me about my reactions? How do you want me to respond?" Record what he says. Choose to repent of improper responses and say "Yes, Lord" to what He is speaking to you.

ENDNOTE

[1] Bill Johnson, http://bjm.org

CHAPTER 11

The Faith to Move Mountains

MATTHEW 17

When they came to the crowd, a man approached Jesus and knelt before him. "Lord, have mercy on my son," he said. "He has seizures and is suffering greatly. He often falls into the fire or into the water. I brought him to your disciples, but they could not heal him." "You unbelieving and perverse genera-tion," Jesus replied, "how long shall I stay with you? How long shall I put up with you? Bring the boy here to me." Jesus rebuked the demon, and it came out of the boy, and he was healed at that moment. Then the disciples came to Jesus in private and asked, "Why couldn't we drive it out?" He replied, "Because you have so little faith. Truly I tell you, if you have faith as small as a mustard seed, you can say to this mountain, 'Move from here to there,' and it will move. Nothing will be impossible for you." MATTHEW 17:14-20

Not sure if you know this, but the Dutch have the most faith of any people group. Yup, all of the mountains in Holland have been cast into the sea. Not my best joke, but it does introduce the premise of this chapter.

It would appear that we don't have to have lots of faith for us to get into the Faith Zone. Jesus said a tiny bit of faith, a mustard seed-sized faith, is enough to move mountains and, by implication, any other obstacle that gets in our way. In the previous chapter we noted that a Gentile mother from Lebanon had this precise revelation. She knew that a crumb was enough to get her demonized daughter set free. While others needed Jesus to come to their home, to touch them, to calm storms, she just needed a tiny crumb. Jesus said that she had great faith.

As we look at this passage from Matthew 17, we see the Twelve lacked this revelation. Nine of the Twelve were rebuked. Jesus tells them that they are in the "little faith" category. Let's take a closer look at this story and what we can learn from it.

MOUNTAIN GLORY AND VALLEY TRIALS

Jesus has just had another amazing experience with his Father as he is on an unnamed mountain, along with Peter, James, and John. Glory manifested.

> There he was transfigured before them. His face shone like the sun, and his clothes became as white as the light. Just then there appeared before them Moses and Elijah, talking with Jesus. MATTHEW 17:2-3

The three disciples would have been amazed. I am quite sure that Jesus was also having a good day. God's presence came down onto that mountain and transformed Jesus. His countenance was changed by God's glory. We have a small glimpse into what heaven will be like.

We don't know how long they were on this mountain or even where it is in Israel. What we do know is that when they rejoined the disciples a small crowd had gathered. The people presumably knew that at some point Jesus would be back. The people had a positive expectation that good things would happen if they waited long enough. In that group is a very desperate father. His son has epilepsy and experiences frequent seizures that threaten his life. The father explains the need of his son to the nine disciples who are also waiting for Jesus. The father asks them to heal his son. His son's life is in the balance; the boy needs to be healed now.

EPILEPSY

Epilepsy is a terrible disease. The word *epilepsy* literally means *seizure*. Something possesses the person, and in a worst-case scenario, shakes them. While there are no known reasons for this disease, it is listed as neurological in nature. Some people challenged with epilepsy have very little abnormalities. Some have such violent attacks that it puts their very lives at risk.

People often inflict injury on themselves during a seizure. Some choke as they swallow their tongue. It is not a nice thing to witness seizures, let alone to suffer from them. We had a lady who used to attend our church who suffered from epilepsy. She wore an ice hockey helmet. Her attacks were so frequent and so violent that she often knocked herself out while falling to the ground. Several times in our meetings she had episodes that lasted upwards of fifteen seconds. Very scary.

The boy in this narrative appears to be in the extreme range. The demons behind the seizures were trying to kill him. They would trigger the epilepsy when the boy was near water and fire. You can imagine the urgency in the father's tone as he begged Jesus to do something. Jesus did something very unique. Instead of ministering to this boy, he rebuked the nine disciples right in front of the father and son. Usually, the rebukes were private. Perhaps as Jesus' ministry was drawing to a close he had less time for his team, who were still not getting it.

Either way, Jesus confronted them. *"You unbelieving and perverse generation,"* Jesus replied, *"how long shall I stay with you? How long shall I put up with you?"* (Matthew 17:17).

DELIVERANCE MINISTRY

The Twelve's inability to minister freedom frustrated Jesus. He expected that they should be able to handle this kind of challenge by that point. He had already released them in pairs to heal the sick and cast out demons (Matthew 10:1). We know that the 70 who were later sent out in pairs positively reported their ability to heal and to also free people from spirits (Luke 10:17). What I find interesting is the confidence that Jesus had in the Twelve's ability to drive out spirits. There are no stories in the Old Testament of anyone being able to do this. Now, because of the anointing, every believer in Jesus can.

The first person to be cleansed of a demon in the history of mankind is an unnamed man in Capernaum. You'll remember the man interrupted Jesus while He was preaching (Mark 1:23-24). His restoration leads to the first revival meeting, later that evening (Mark 1:32-34).

In Jesus' first recorded sermon, which he gave in Nazareth, he uses Isaiah 61 as his text (Luke 4:17–19). He makes the clear statement that he having recently been anointed by Father God at his baptism, is now able to set captives free. The people of his synagogue took great offence at this statement and sought to stone Him immediately. Jesus was very convinced that bringing freedom to people was a function of the anointing.

Many stories record that spirits left people at the ministry of Jesus. My rough estimation is that one-third of all the healings of Jesus involved some level of deliverance. Deliverance had become customary in the ministry of Jesus.

People came to Jesus purely for this purpose. The Canaanite lady was one such person. She travelled south from modern day Lebanon into Galilee to find Jesus so her daughter could be delivered (Matthew 15:21–22).

REBUKE OF THE DISCIPLES

Jesus expected that his Twelve could also minister deliverance. We know that they had witnessed thousands of people set free. This was not new for them. Yet the nine disciples couldn't free this epileptic boy. Jesus was frustrated and called his men *"unbelieving and perverse."* A harsh rebuke. *Perverse* implies that they were twisted in some way. They knew what to do but didn't want to do it. They had what it takes but lacked the will to follow through.

I'd like to focus on the statement Jesus made about the disciple's unbelief.

What is it that they didn't believe? How had their twisted thinking so negatively affected their ability to do what Jesus knew they could do?

> *"Bring the boy here to me." Jesus rebuked the demon, and it came out of the*
> *boy, and he was healed at that moment.* MATTHEW 17:17-18

Jesus takes over in an almost matter-of-fact way. He kicks the demon
out of the young boy and his epilepsy is gone. He was instantly healed.
Amazing.

Spoiler alert: later in this chapter I have an incredible testimony of one
of my friends who had the very same experience. She had twelve seizures a day.

The parallel passage, in Mark 9:25, tells us that Jesus ministered to the
boy in an urgent manner. He did this to protect the father and son from
the eyes of the crowd. His care for people is evident. We also read that
those who did witness the interaction with the boy thought that Jesus had
somehow killed him, because he looked dead (Mark 9:26). I believe he was
simply "out in the spirit." I've seen thousands of people out in the spirit,
so a person lying on a floor is not an unusual sight for me. But it was new
to the locals who observed this deliverance. They were not sure what had
happened. That is until the boy got up, completely healed.

The reaction of the disciples afterwards is very telling. Perhaps a bit put
out by the public rebuke, they came to Jesus later to find out why they
were unable to help the boy. *"Then the disciples came to Jesus in private and
asked, 'Why couldn't we drive it out?'"* Matthew 17:19.

LITTLE FAITH

The answer from Jesus is simple and to the point: *"He replied, 'Because you have so little faith'"* Matthew 17:20. Jesus doesn't say that they have no faith, but little faith. After almost three years of watching Jesus cast out thousands of spirits, the spirit in this boy should not have posed a problem. All they needed was to act in faith on what they knew, but this is the very thing that they didn't do.

As we have looked at the various stories from Matthew, I trust you are agreeing with me that faith is the process of acting on a revelation. So was the problem for these nine men that they didn't know something? Or is it that they didn't act on what they knew? I believe it was the latter. They clearly knew that Jesus could free people from spirits. They had witnessed it over and over again. Presumably they had at least once, on their first ministry trip, done the same. So the issue was not revelation, it was the action part that they got wrong.

Did the spirit in this boy intimidate them? Why were they not able to step into the doing part of faith?

LEARNING DELIVERANCE MINISTRY THE HARD WAY

In the late 1980s, I was an assistant pastor at the largest Baptist church in Scarborough, the eastern part of Toronto. We were a large multicultural congregation. We didn't believe that demons were real. One particular Monday I had to drop in at the church office, which was about a three-minute drive from our home. It was my day off. While I was there to pick something up, our receptionist asked if I could take a phone call from one of the ladies in our congregation. I did.

The lady told me that her husband was demon possessed and that he was cursing her. She needed me to come over to her home right away. My first thought was *why me?* Then another idea came to me: *I've done this before; it won't be too hard. I can go and be home before Sandra misses me.*

I remembered when I was 16 years of age and a counsellor at a Christian kid's camp. One of my rebellious cabin kids had given his life to Jesus. That very night, while sharing his testimony at the campfire with all the rest of the campers, a spirit took over his body. He freaked everyone out. He was cursing in a man's deep voice. He thrashed violently and scared the other camp kids, many who were much younger. Several of us counsellors tackled him and dragged him back to the bunkhouse.

The guest missionary of the week, who knew that my parents had been missionaries in Malawi, Africa, assumed that I would know what to do. I didn't. But because this kid was in my cabin, and no one else knew what to do, I took the lead. My recollection is that the two other counsellors where holding this twelve or thirteen-year-old boy on his bed to stop his flailing. He cursed us repeatedly. I did not know what do to, but being a strategic person, I came up with a plan.

I asked the demon who was swearing at us how many spirits were in the boy. "Fifty." Okay then. I commanded demon number 50 to leave. Then number 49. Then number 48. One by one I counted backwards. As we got to single digit numbers, the negative manifestations began to increase. He screamed, thrashed about, and heat was coming off his body. It was getting very intense. When I commanded number one to leave, everything changed. The boy was back to his normal self and wondered why there were three men on his bunk holding him down. He had no recollection of what had just happened.

So, with this one and only deliverance session in mind, I headed to the home to free this husband so I could go back to enjoying my day off. It turned out not to be as easy as that.

When I arrived the lady greeted me and pointed to her husband. He was sitting in his white underwear on the couch and jeering at me. He began to mock me and tell me to go ahead and try to free him. And that is exactly what I tried to do. I commanded the demons in him to stop manifesting. They didn't. I commanded the spirits to leave. They didn't. I bound them. That didn't work either.

I quickly realized that I was in way over my head on this one. The spirits in this man mocked me with every attempt, with every prayer, and with every command. Sadly, the lady realized that this pastor wasn't able to help her. I came to the same conclusion.

PHILIP PHILIPS

As I realized I was out of my depth, I had a thought. God stepped in and graciously reminded me of a guest speaker I had in one of my Seminary classes. Philip Philips had talked to the graduating class about career opportunities as chaplains. Philip oversaw the Protestant chapels in all of Canada's airports.

I remember that he had mentioned in his class that from time to time he had to free people from spirits. He was the only one that I knew of who seemed to do this kind of thing on a regular basis. I called him and he agreed to come to the home within the hour. I told the wife that a specialist was coming over. I sat in a chair waiting while the husband mocked me, swore at me, and gloated that he had won the battle. It was a long hour.

A car came into the driveway and something interesting happened. The man instantly became agitated. When Mr. Philips knocked on the door, the man began to cower like a dog that's been beaten too many times. My recollection is that when Philip walked in the door, the man began to curl up in the fetal position. I introduced Philip to the lady. She thanked him for coming, as did I. Philip calmly walked over to the man and commanded all the spirits to leave him immediately. There was a mild convulsion and he was free.

The man was grateful for Philip's ministry. His wife thanked Philip. I thanked Philip. Philip and I walked out to our cars together. I debriefed with Philip in the driveway. I told him that I had said the very same prayer that he had just uttered, but nothing had happened. Why?

Philip turned to me and said something very simple.
"You didn't believe your prayer."
Ouch. But he was right. I walked into the situation with bravado. I hadn't

prayed, I had little experience, and apparently no authority. I was like the nine disciples whom Jesus rebuked. Little faith.

I had revelation that I could free the man. In fact, I had prior history of doing just that. But in the face of greater opposition, my confidence waivered. Doubt built up. The problem wasn't the truth; the problem was me acting in what I knew. The nine disciples were the problem. They hit a wall bigger than their confidence. They had little faith.

> *"Truly I tell you, if you have faith as small as a mustard seed, you can say to this mountain, 'Move from here to there,' and it will move. Nothing will be impossible for you."* MATTHEW 17:20

To further answer their question, Jesus said that *small* is really all you need. However, it wasn't just revelation that the nine disciples needed. The *small* revelation they had was good enough if joined with action. Little faith can move a mountain. These nine disciples apparently had tried to free the boy. I'm guessing that they had said things like "out," "be free," etc. But nothing changed and they gave up.

PRAYER AND FASTING

The King James translation of Matthew 17:21 and the parallel passage in Mark 9:29 give us another clue. Jesus adds the bit about "fasting." Two points on this one.

First, the word *fasting* is not in the Greek text. It has been added by well-meaning people. I'm assuming scholars, who knew that fasting gives us greater power·and authority, would have added the word. The translators' theology guided them to "help" the text make sense.

Second, I believe Jesus does imply the concept of fasting. Fasting is a discipline. Jesus only fasted once that we know of: immediately following his baptism. However, he taught that others should fast.

I believe Jesus was teaching his disciples that just saying the word *out* doesn't always work. Prayer is more than mere words. What Jesus was saying was "keep praying, don't give up." Some challenges are not so simple. They are spiritual battles, where we are actually the ones tested. Battles reveal what we have revelation for. I can say I believe that demons will leave people through prayer. But when I was the one confronted by a man sitting in his white underwear and manifesting demons, it was a different scenario. Did I act according to what I believed?

This is where the nine men got stuck. It is where I got stuck visiting that husband in Scarborough. Talk is easy. Acting out what we know is quite different. The good news is this: even with a beginner's understanding of the authority we have over sickness, demons, lack of finances, addictions, etc., we can overcome. We don't have to know everything in order to be effective in ministry.

Little knowledge is generally what children have. They don't have all the truths about God that adults do. But they believe what they know. That is why Jesus said we have to have the faith of a child to enter the kingdom of heaven (Matthew 18:2–4). We get to function in kingdom activities just like Jesus did. We get to be used by God to see great miracles happen because of our little faith. I love it.

Chloe Glassborough, along with her husband, Stuart, are on the senior apostolic leadership team for Catch The Fire worldwide. Chloe is someone who functions at a high level of kingdom activities, and has great faith. Her story is all the more remarkable considering how broken she was in the past. I've asked Chloe to tell her story in her own. Here she goes.

STORY OF CHLOE GLASSBOROUGH

For many years I longed to be able to love. As all children do, I needed to feel loved but I struggled daily with a deep sense of abandonment, like I didn't fit in and I could not find where I belonged. I didn't fully understand love or the concept of loving. My life had been full of highs and lows, with a great deal of emotional pain along with desperation to be "normal," whatever normal was. I was desperate to be free from pain and to experience the love of God in all of his fullness. Clearly, I had no idea of how that would happen and what it would look like.

So what's my story?

I had experiences growing up that made me believe I was unlovable, unworthy, and not "good for anything." I grew up without the influence of a loving father, and this led to many painful memories and hurts that I based my life on for many years. I had so many unanswered questions and so many unspoken thoughts. What is love? What does the completeness of love look like? Was I worthy of love? What did I do wrong to deserve the pain I experienced? What is family? What does vulnerability look like in a safe place?

Understanding being loved and the concept of loving someone freely was a daily battle for me, amidst the pain of living in shame and daily torment. Sadly, this turned to deep bitterness, hatred, and unforgiveness in my heart.

But one day, Love found me!

Between the age of 9 and 27, my life entered a season that felt like suffocation at a completely new level. I became closely acquainted with sickness. I would go as far as to say sickness became my friend, sickness became my identity, and sickness took over my life.

I developed epilepsy and was finally diagnosed at age ten, in March 1987. I went through several years in primary school of having what are called "high-level absences." These are the occurrence of an abrupt, transient loss or impairment of consciousness. I was having roughly twelve of these daily, and they were getting worse. When I was diagnosed there was not much known about epilepsy, other than the distinction of petit mal and grand mal seizures. I was diagnosed with petit mal and put on a high dose of Epilog medication to control the number of seizures I was experiencing. It did not work. Epilepsy is often caused by a trauma of some kind, but often the precise cause is unknown. It wasn't until 1995 that doctors found a medication that really worked.

I remember one of the first episodes I ever had. We were at our end-of-term Christmas concert at school. I was so excited to be playing the clarinet after many Saturday mornings spent at music school. I was actually really good! I recall the hush as seven o'clock came; the large oak hall became a place of tension and silence, as each parent waited eagerly for their "little one" to wow the audience with their young talent. I remember being sad that all my friends were talking about "mum and dad" who had come to listen to them and how proud they would be. I felt so sad, and in my brokenness I started to panic with the shame and embarrassment of being associated with a "dad" in a psychiatric hospital. I was yanked out of that place of despair as the teachers opened the door for us all to walk in to the hall and take our places. I could smell Christmas, the pine and cinnamon scent that surround a tree and that I associated with all Christmas decorations. I remember breathing in deeply as I started to walk towards the door. That is the last thing I remember, until three minutes later.

Without knowing what was happening I went into an episode—an absence. My eyes went blank and everything switched off, but my body kept working as normal. All sense of clarity in hearing and sight vanished. I walked straight through the entire row of chairs where my classmates were going to be sitting. I walked straight through all the music stands and towards the wall; I was completely disorientated and distressed. The realization of what had just happened suddenly came to my mind as the absence ceased. I faced the wall feeling hot, my head pounding, and riddled with shame, embarrassed that my amazing opportunity to make my mummy proud had just been overtaken by epilepsy.

Sadly, these things happened frequently and the seizures were not controlled. As time progressed, the neurologist continued to increase my medication dosage, which made school difficult. During these absences I recall missing many critical parts of my education. I looked normal but would be completely switched off to the world around me. I could feel things but not stop myself from moving, often having no control over my actions and hurting myself in the process. I would "zone out" of conversations and miss half of what was being said. This repeated at regular intervals throughout the course of any given day.

The stigma associated with epilepsy in those days was terrible. No one really understood the disease and many of my peers teased me with names like "mental" or "retard." This tore at my heart and fractured my psyche. At the time, my dad was in a psychiatric hospital himself, so all I remember was saying to Mum, "Am I going to end up like him?" It must have been heartbreaking for Mum to see the pain and fear in my eyes. As if life with family dysfunction wasn't hard enough, epilepsy made things worse. We were out of our depth and still sinking.

The seizures got progressively worse, and we reached a crisis point as the neurologist I was seeing at the time said he had done all he could do. He would sign me off to remain on this medication, which was frightening because it did nothing to control the seizures.

At a family member's recommendation, I went to see a specialist at Maudsley Epilepsy hospital. I remember sitting in the clinic waiting room. The smells of disinfectant and of sick and needy children were hard to bear, especially because I associated hospitals with fear because of my Dad. Children afflicted by epilepsy sat in wheelchairs, unable to function.

Some children sat silent and expressionless in the corner on the chair, while I sat riddled with fear of the unknown and held my mummy's hand. I wondered if I was going to end up like that.

We were called into the consultant's room and the kind eyes of the "grandpa" that looked at me secured my heart, banished my fear, and brought complete ease and rest to my soul. This doctor really cared about his profession and really cared about my family. I could tell he was aware of our family situation and he went out of his way to reassure both my mum and me. He asked me to describe what it was like to have a seizure. I told him how my body reacted, how over the years the absence had progressed to body convulsions. Sometimes they were twitches and sometimes they were worse. I explained how the pain in my head would develop before a seizure, and my eyes felt abnormal.

There was one time when I had been home alone, when had I stood up and had to find a door to hold onto to steady myself because I could feel my body starting to twitch. I missed the door handle and hit my head on the door and collapsed to the ground. I had no idea how long I was there. When I came around, I was in tears, disoriented and confused. The last thing I remembered was being on my bed. Now I was in a heap on the floor in the entrance hall, with a pounding headache, feeling frightened. Mum was working at school and I was at home, there wasn't any other option, she couldn't watch me 24/7. When she came home and saw what happened, she was overwhelmed by guilt that she hadn't been there. After a seizure I was usually very tired—I would sleep for a long time and go into a bit of a haze. Life was not great and we couldn't carry on like that.

After this description, the doctor said he had some good news.

"I think I know the type of Epilepsy you have."

I remember saying, "Yes, so do we. Petit Mal?"

"No. I need to confirm with a scan. But there are over 40 types of epilepsy. You need an EEG (Electroencephalogram) to confirm my findings."

An electroencephalogram (EEG) is a recording of brain activity. The brain's cells produce tiny electrical signals when they send messages to each other. During an EEG, small electrodes are placed on to your scalp. They pick up your brain's electrical signals and send them to a machine called an electroencephalograph, which records the signals as wavy lines onto a computer screen or paper. The pattern of electrical activity produced on an EEG can be used to help diagnose a number of conditions that affect the brain. This would help the doctor confirm his theory.

I needed to be put to sleep for one of the tests to check for evidence of seizures in my sleep.

I felt unsure and fearful about what people would say if they knew my brain was being tested, and my heart began to sadden at the thought of more blood tests, different medications, and longer spells at hospitals.

The probes were placed all over my head as I sat in a dark room on a hospital bed. Various tests were carried out, including having flashing lights placed in front of my eyes to see the brain's reaction when suddenly met with such a stark contrast.

For many years, I had been on high-level drugs and very drowsy, but that day they found answers! I was diagnosed with severe Myoclonic seizures, which are shock-like jerks of a muscle or group of muscles. Immediately I was placed on a new medication and over time the seizures started to be controlled. I was put on a very high dose, so I was extremely sleepy, to the point of near-sedation.

Despite the tiredness and the stigma, I was determined to succeed at something! With the seizures getting better, my love and ability for sports increased. As an athlete I trained hard and I understood the level of persistence required to get my stamina to increase over a period of time to bring me to a place of victory at whatever sport I laid my hand to. I often trained through the pain barrier, holding on with gritted teeth towards the goal in front of me. No matter how much my muscles cried out for me to rest, I knew the fruit of that moment would be critical to the destiny of that day in sporting season. Little did I know that one day I would need to simply live these values as daily choices to even be able to lift my leg, get out of bed, or walk across the room!

I was so determined to achieve something that my tenacity for achievement became my worst enemy in my teenage years. I trained very hard at many sports, with abandonment and bitterness as my driving forces. I wanted to prove to myself and others that I was good at something and worth being celebrated. I think that's called performance.

One day my knees started to hurt and crunch, and the pain got worse and worse. I was referred to a consultant and diagnosed with Chondro-malacia patellae (also known as CMP). CMP is an abnormal softening of the cartilage of the underside the kneecap. It causes pain in the front of the knee. CMP is one of the most common causes of chronic knee pain and results from degeneration of cartilage due to poor alignment of the kneecap as it slides over the lower end of the thighbone. This process is sometimes referred to as patellofemoral syndrome.

The pain got so bad as I entered my twenties that I was told if I didn't have an operation, I would be in a wheelchair by the time I reached the age of 30. By this time, I was engaged to Stu, my husband, but our engagement was overshadowed by sickness. I was offered a procedure called the Elmslie Trillate procedure, one of a number of procedures known as "distal realignment procedures," in which the kneecap is repositioned by realigning the attachment of the patellar tendon (tendon under the kneecap) to the underlying tibial tubercle. The operation was to prevent the kneecap going too far over to one side (subluxation) or jumping completely out of its groove (dislocation). I had two 3-inch bolts placed through my knee to keep it aligned, and 7 inches of Quadricep (thigh) muscle cut in each leg to release the strain on my knee. During this season my determination to succeed in sport was necessary to push past the pain of everyday movements. Having both legs out of action, one of which was in plaster from hip to ankle, was debilitating and frustrating.

Was I ever going to be free from pain? Was I ever going to stop being "an issue"? It was a long journey of relearning how to walk, but sadly, the operation was not as successful as they had hoped. The pain was debilitating. Stu had to carry me upstairs, and I would come downstairs on my bottom one step at a time. I needed Stu to help me put my shoes on, get in and out of the car, and simply care for me.

Along with the above limitations, I had a lactose sensitivity. This meant that when I ate anything containing lactose I would either feel sick, have diarrhoea, or extreme stomach cramps. This is not great at any time, but when you love food it's worse—especially when you love ice cream and cheese!

We reached a new level of desperation one day when I woke up with a migraine. I had a migraine that lasted for six months, that fed off itself, called a transformed migraine. Transformed migraines are chronic, daily head-aches with a vascular quality (meaning that they are throbbing in nature). They need to be intercepted early on if the cycle is to be broken. Sadly, we did not receive our specialist appointment quickly enough. For six months I woke up and went to bed with a horrendous throbbing headache.

As you can gather my health was not the greatest. I had lived with pain, hospitals, sickness, and shame from the age of ten. My home life as a child was not good; fear of my father was the emotion that we lived and breathed daily. Something needed to change quickly if Stu and I were to have any kind of "normality" in our lives.

Our pastor at the time suggested we go to a "Father Loves You" confer-ence at Bath City Church in England. It was March 2003. Stu "hated" Charismatics, and I hated the word *father*. So we decided to go to the "Father Loves You" conference, run by Charismatics! We still laugh today wondering how on earth we decided to go. I was determined not to cry, and kept saying how fine I was and didn't need this conference. Stu just analysed everything; as a scientist (Stu is veterinary surgeon, by trade) he couldn't get his head around anything to do with God moving in power and healing people.

I was desperate inside for any kind of breakthrough. I needed pain to leave our life. We needed a touch from the King. I had loved Jesus since I was a little girl, but hated the thought of having a Father in Heaven. He would just be like my earthly father.

John Arnott (whom we had never met) took to the platform on the first day of the conference and spoke about the Father's love and forgiveness. The room was packed with some 1,700 people. There was a buzz of expectation in the atmosphere and I couldn't stop crying from the moment I walked into the auditorium. As I heard about a Father who loved me, who loved me just for me, who wouldn't harm me, but loved me unconditionally—I completely broke emotionally! I was desperate to receive that kind of love. My heart felt amazing and I knew I had encountered a love that I was designed to live and experience all my life. I instantly felt secure, peaceful, happy, relieved, and hungry for more of this amazing Father. I forgave my biological father from my heart for the first time and yelled out loud, "You owe me nothing," I gave up being a victim, and exchanged that for my position as a daughter of the King. This brought an instant shift in my mindset about who I was and where I was called to be.

The following session was a call forward for worship leaders. I went forward ready for an impartation. I thought, *Yes, this is a good alter call to respond to. I won't have to cry; I can just receive!* I remember standing in the lines ready to receive everything God had for me in those moments, to take me to the next level of worship leading.

I had my eyes closed and a lady put her hands on me and started to pray for me. I felt heavy and fell to the ground. She stayed with me for ages.

I felt heat all over my body, and started to tremble. The lady said, "I see the same glory on you as was on Moses when he came down the mountain!" The heat got more intense all over my body and in my head and stomach. Then she said, "Receive your healing."

I thought, *Wow, how does she know I am sick?* Suddenly, I felt all the pain start to lift from my body and my head got clearer and the throbbing stopped. The stomach pain ceased, the knee pain went.

I yelled, "I think I am healed," and the lady helped me to my feet. It was Carol Arnott. I said to her, "I think I am healed, the pain has gone."

She asked a few questions and got me up to the platform. I couldn't remember the last time I had walked up stairs—and I just walked up to the platform. Stu was back in the seats and couldn't believe what he was seeing. John interviewed me and asked me to kneel down—so I did! I jumped up and down on my knees. NO PAIN!! WOO HOOO! No pain, no headache, no tummy ache! I felt full of love and completely healed.

I ate cheese and mayonnaise, plus some cream, on my return trip to test if the lactose intolerance was healed, and it was. No reaction, no pain, no diarrhoea, I was healed!

With this in mind, we visited the doctor on our way back and I showed her that my knees were healed. I told her about all the other ailments that had disappeared. I told her that I felt it was time to reduce the epilepsy medication because I was healed. She told me I would be crazy to come off the drugs as I have been on anticonvulsant medication since I was ten years old. I was so sad, as I knew that the Lord had healed me completely.

The doctor then looked at Stu and she said, "Well I guess since you are a veterinary surgeon, here's what we will do. You need to track Chloe closely and come in every month for the next year. We will reduce her medication by 25 mg every month for the next year. If there are any signs of twitches or seizures, you must go back onto the full dose."

Within a year, I had reduced the drugs and came to the day of the last tablet. It was the most amazing feeling. I was fine, I was well, I was seizure-free!

Now though, I didn't really know who I was meant to be. My identity had been wrapped up in sickness and medication for seventeen years. The Lord had completely healed me, so who was I now? I began to discover who it was that I really was. Stu felt he had a new wife—I didn't stop talking now! I got involved in many things again; I could ski and do all the things I thought I would never be able to do.

At that conference in March 2003, I chose life, I chose to step into grace, I chose love, I chose to live a lifestyle of forgiveness, and I chose to be Fathered by the World's Greatest Dad. This first encounter released a tenacity in our hearts to serve our Heavenly Father and dedicate the rest of our lives to seeing people healed, restored, and set free from the pain and heartache that can bind and cripple them. We were at a place of emotional and physical exhaustion, but the breakthrough came in our little decision and choice, and ended up changing our lives forever.

GOING DEEPER

1. Is there a demonic stronghold that you struggle with? A bad temper, lying, stealing, criticism, jealousy, etc.? Ask the Lord where this began in your life.

2. Repent for giving this stronghold a foothold in your life. Forgive the people who negatively contributed to this stronghold. State your intention to now respond in Godly ways, rather than demonic ways, and state what these Godly opposite ways are (you don't move from darkness to neutral, you move from darkness to living in the light). State this new light that you will now live in. This lets the demons know they will no longer be entertained within you and it is in their best interests to leave.

3. Renounce the spirit that empowers the stronghold and ask the Lord to separate you from any negative power that Satan has over your life. Welcome the Holy Spirit to set up new ownership and management in this area of your life.

CHAPTER 12

Jesus Lived by Faith

JOHN 5

Somehow, I believed an inaccurate teaching about Jesus for much of my life. I was taught, accepted, and held to the view that Jesus was the divine Son of God. Let me explain.

I do believe that Jesus is the divine Son of God, but what was inaccurate was the idea that Jesus functioned in his divinity while living on planet earth. I don't believe that any more. What I believe is that Jesus was both human and divine while living on earth two millennia ago. Paul calls him the *"the man Christ Jesus"* (1 Timothy 2:5).

To clarify even more, I believe that Jesus chose to live exclusively in his humanity. Even while divine, Jesus never tapped into his God-abilities, but chose to experience humanity in all its forms. There are many passages of Scripture that speak to this. I somehow missed them in my early years of following Jesus. Perhaps the clearest is Paul's explanation in Philippians 2. We'll get to that in a moment.

JESUS DIDN'T LIVE AS GOD ON PLANET EARTH

The problem of believing that Jesus functioned in his divinity is threefold.

First, it goes against the teaching of Paul, John, Matthew, and Jesus himself. Second, it subtly lowers our expectancy for the miraculous in our lives. Third, it nullifies living in faith and being led by the Holy Spirit.

If Jesus did all his supernatural works, the healing and miracles, as the divine Son of God, it means that we can't ever expect to do the same unless we too are divine. That is how I grew up. I knew that Jesus was amazing. He walked on water. He multiplied food. He healed the sick and raised the dead. I can't do any of those things because I'm not a god.

Well, it turns out I can and should be doing those things. Jesus himself prophesied over all of our lives. *"Very truly I tell you, whoever believes in me will do the works I have been doing, and they will do even greater things than these, because I am going to the Father"* (John 14:12). We don't have to be gods to do God-stuff, we simply need to be anointed and living in faith.

Jesus lived by faith as an example for us. He needed to have his Father reveal things to him in order to enter the Faith Zone. The Spirit of Father God, the Holy Spirit, led Jesus. Jesus showed how easy it is to function in the miraculous.

JESUS CALLED HIMSELF THE SON OF MAN

The gospel authors, Matthew, Mark, Luke, and John, use the phrase "son of man" a total of 78 times to refer to Jesus. They use the phrase "son of God" twenty-two times. I believe this is deliberate and intentional. Of the twenty-two mentions of "son of God," eight are statements from Satan, demons, and angels. Most of the other references are from Jesus' critics. Jesus only uses this title to describe himself once (John 5:25). The writers are clearly telling us that while Jesus is the son of God, he is also very human.

PAUL'S REVELATION ABOUT JESUS

I used to believe that Jesus functioned with all his godly attributes while on earth. I was taught in my Seminary that Jesus was omniscient (all-knowing), omnipresent (everywhere all at once), and omnipotent (all-powerful). Those are his skill sets as the Son of God, as the co-creator of this world. But Paul is deliberate in telling us that Jesus didn't use these attributes while living with us.

Who, being in very nature God, did not consider equality with God something to be used to his own advantage; rather, he made himself nothing by taking the very nature of a servant, being made in human likeness. And being found in appearance as a man, he humbled himself by becoming obedient to death—even death on a cross. PHILIPPIANS 2:6-8

Paul makes it very clear. Jesus is God: *"being in very nature God"* (Philippians 2:6). There is no question about this. Jesus made an amazing choice. While He had the right to live in his God-qualities and attributes, He didn't hold onto them. He let them go, for a season. *"Did not consider equality with God something to be used to his own advantage"* (Philippians 2:7).

Jesus' choice was to completely identify with us as mortals. *"Taking the very nature of a servant, being made in human likeness"* (Philippians 2:8). Amazing.

One of my theories is that for every doctrinal statement in the Bible, there is at least one corresponding story that illustrates the fact. So, are there stories that clearly show that Jesus wasn't everywhere at once? Or that Jesus wasn't knowledgeable in all details of this universe? Was Jesus able to do anything he wanted, any time of the day?

Thank you for asking. Yes, there are many stories that show that Jesus didn't live as God while on earth.

JESUS IN HIS EARTHLY SUIT — NOT OMNIPRESENT

Clearly, Jesus in his humanity was only in one place at a time. There are no stories in the Gospels of Jesus being in two places at once. He was limited to time and space just like we are. That was His choice. Jesus also made an interesting statement to the Twelve just before the cross. Do you remember His teaching on the topics of His Father and the Holy Spirit in John 14—16?

One of his words was this: *"But very truly I tell you, it is for your good that I am going away. Unless I go away, the Advocate will not come to you; but if I go, I will send him to you"* (John 16:7).

Let me paraphrase what I believe Jesus is saying.

"Men, it is best that I leave. In a few days we aren't going to be living in community. You will soon be ministering all over the known world. I know that each of you would like me to be with you, but I simply can't be in two places at once.

So... I am going to head back to the Father. I will send someone who is able to be with each of you wherever you are. He will be your teacher, comforter, helper, etc. His name is Holy Spirit."

By introducing the Holy Spirit to the disciples, Jesus acknowledged that he was limited to being in one place at a time.

JESUS IN HIS EARTHLY SUIT — NOT OMNISCIENT

Did Jesus know everything? Did he have all information known to humans and God?

In chapter six of this book we looked at a woman who was living in the town of Capernaum. You'll remember that she had a bleeding disorder for twelve years that very negatively affected her life. She had spent all of her money on doctors and still things were getting worse. She acted on the simple revelation that she was given by Father God. She touched the hem of Jesus' garment and was instantly healed. She got her miracle. Do you remember Jesus's reaction? "*'Who touched me?' Jesus asked*" (Luke 8:45).

Would an all-knowing, divine Jesus not know who touched him? Either Jesus is lying or what he said was true. The only conclusion I can come up with is that Jesus didn't know the next few minutes of his life in advance.

While he was walking through the crowded streets of Capernaum, it would appear that he was oblivious that a lady was sneaking up through the crowd. He didn't know she was doing this with the sole purpose of getting her healing. What clued Jesus in to the miracle was a change in his physical strength. He felt anointing leave his body. *"But Jesus said, 'Someone touched me; I know that power has gone out from me'"* (Luke 8:46).

Those of you who minster by laying hands on others will know this feeling. It happens often, especially for those who have a healing ministry. The Lord gives me shortcuts. I know to stop praying and get right to checking the healing because I feel these power surges. They are normal for anointed people. This is how Jesus knew that someone had been healed, not prior knowledge.

Let me give you more proof. In chapter three, we looked at the great faith of the Roman centurion. Luke 7:4-5 tells us that he was known as a man who loved the Jewish people. He had paid to build the town's synagogue. When he talked to Jesus about his paralyzed servant, you will remember that Jesus volunteered to go to the home and heal him (Matthew 8:7). The centurion, who is functioning as the chief of police, declines the invite. He asks that Jesus just say the word. He knows something that negates the need to have Jesus come to his home.

Do you remember what his revelation was? *"For I myself am a man under authority"* (Matthew 8:9). What he was saying to Jesus was that both of them were under authority. He was the first person to understand that Jesus was not the one healing people. Rather, Jesus was simply the middleman. God the Father was the one who wanted this healing.

The Holy Spirit was the agent of the healing. Jesus was simply the one facilitating it. Jesus' normal practice was to put the anointing on people via a touch. He would declare the will of God with a command.

But this centurion, with a great revelation, knows that we can skip the house visit today. We are both busy people. Cut to the chase and say the command that you have had from your Father. Jesus did not know that this was going to be the response from this centurion. He was as shocked as the rest of the people. Amazing.

JESUS IN HIS EARTHLY SUIT—NOT OMNIPOTENT

Was Jesus all-powerful when he walked about in Israel two thousand years ago? No. Seven times in John's gospel Jesus tells us that he can't do anything on his own. Jesus was completely dependent on revelation from his Father. If Father God didn't talk to him, show him pictures, or prompt his spirit, Jesus was incapable of acting in the miraculous. Let's look at some of the triggers that motivated Jesus to action.

SEEING

Jesus gave them this answer: "Very truly I tell you, the Son can do nothing by himself; he can do only what he sees his Father doing, because whatever the Father does the Son also does." JOHN 5:19

Jesus couldn't do anything in his humanity. That is, unless his Father showed him something; then Jesus knew what to do. Jesus gave this state-ment as a rebuttal for those who asked why he healed a blind man on the Sabbath. He saw it.

A couple of very interesting words are used in the story of this miracle. Look at the verses below.

> Here a great number of disabled people used to lie—the blind, the lame, the
> paralyzed. One who was there had been an invalid for thirty-eight years. When
> Jesus saw him lying there and learned that he had been in this condition for a
> long time, he asked him, "Do you want to get well?" JOHN 5:5-6

Does the fact that Jesus *saw* and *learned* now take on new meaning? I'd like to suggest that this man stood out from the rest of those needing a miracle. Perhaps Jesus had had a dream about this man the night before?

It is possible that the learning Jesus received was simply by asking others who were there to tell him about the blind man. But it is also very probable that Jesus got his information straight from his Father. If my theory is cor-rect, this miracle took place because of Jesus' faith. He had a picture, per-haps a dream, of the man. He knew exactly what that meant. When he now sees the man in person, Jesus jumps into action. Jesus was living by faith.

HEARING

> By myself I can do nothing; I judge only as I hear, and my judgement is just, for
> I seek not to please myself but him who sent me. JOHN 5:30

Again, Jesus says that he was incapable of performing the supernatural unless he had direction. This time he was referring to the process of hearing Father God.

KNOWING

Then Jesus, still teaching in the temple courts, cried out, "Yes, you know me, and you know where I am from. I am not here on my own authority, but he who sent me is true. You do not know him, but I <u>know</u> him because I am from him and he sent me." JOHN 7:28-29

Jesus' authority also came from a knowing of what his Father's will was. I would put this into the spirit category. Our knower isn't in our brain, rather in our spirit, where God's spirit converses directly with us. We don't know why, but we know that we know.

"I have much to say in judgement of you. But he who sent me is trustworthy, and what I have <u>heard</u> from him I tell the world"... So Jesus said, "When you have lifted up the Son of Man, then you will know that I am he and that I do nothing on my own but speak just what the Father has <u>taught</u> me." JOHN 8:26, 28

These two verses include hearing and knowing. Again, Jesus says that he can only communicate what has first been communicated to him.

"I am telling you what I have <u>seen</u> in the Father's presence, and you are doing what you have heard from your father ... As it is, you are looking for a way to kill me, a man who has told you the truth that I <u>heard</u> from God." JOHN 8:38, 40

These verses are how Jesus responded to the Jews who consistently dis-liked him talking about his relationship with Father God. This time Jesus uses the words *sees* and *hears*.

> *For I did not speak on my own, but the Father who sent me commanded me to say all that I have spoken. I know that his command leads to eternal life. So whatever I say is just what the Father has <u>told</u> me to say."* JOHN 12:49–50

The Pharisees continually challenged the authority of Jesus and demand-ed reasons for the things he said. Jesus clarified for them again how he received his revelations: by hearing. He said what he was told to say.

GOD REVEALS HIS DESIRES THROUGH COMPASSION

Compassion is another way in which Jesus received revelation. Compassion is a very interesting feeling that apparently is more than just an emotion. It is also a revelatory expression of God's heart. Below are four passages from Matthew's account of the life of Jesus. Three times Matthew says that compassion was the motivation for Jesus' actions. In one of them, Jesus actually used the word *compassion* to explain why he performed a miracle.

> *When he saw the crowds, he had <u>compassion</u> on them, because they were harassed and helpless, like sheep without a shepherd.* MATTHEW 9:36

> *When Jesus landed and saw a large crowd, he had <u>compassion</u> on them and healed their sick.* MATTHEW 14:14

Jesus called his disciples to him and said, "I have <u>compassion</u> for these people; they have already been with me three days and have nothing to eat. I do not want to send them away hungry, or they may collapse on the way."
MATTHEW 15:32

Jesus had <u>compassion</u> on them and touched their eyes. Immediately they received their sight and followed him. MATTHEW 20:34

Compassion is that feeling we get when we see someone and think, *that isn't right.*

Injustice wells up in us and instead of walking by and doing nothing, we are drawn by our Father into doing something. God speaks to us through this emotion. Once we sense compassion, we have the option of acting or not doing anything. If we act, we move into the Faith Zone where miracles happen.

You will know this emotion well. When we see a beggar asking for change, most of the time we simply walk by. But sometimes, there is a pull. Compassion rises up. We instinctively know that God wants us to give the person some money, to talk to them, to minister to them, etc. God is revealing his heart to us.

So, if Jesus only did things that he saw, heard, or knew, I can be like that. I can see in the spirit. I can hear from my Father. I can know things simply because my spirit has connected with God's spirit. We are wired just like Jesus was. Jesus is our example, our prototype. If Jesus could live this way, so can we. This is awesome news and it means that the Faith Zone is a very real place!

In June of 2015, Sandra and I went to Medellin, Colombia. Two of our friends, Diego and Diana Pineda were starting a Catch The Fire church there. On the drive from the airport to the apartment where we were staying, revelations kicked in without us knowing it. Because of holiday traffic, Diana and our driver, Natalie, decided to take a longer route back into the city. As we drove through winding roads we turned a corner to see that a motorcycle had just crashed. A man and his bike where lying on the road. The accident was beside a restaurant and a few folks had quickly gathered there. One man helped the injured motorcyclist to sit up. Diana and I jumped out of our car and went to pray.

The man was slightly resistant to prayer and as it happened the car behind us had a doctor as a passenger. She quickly took over. As we were walking back to our car, I saw a lady limping. I assumed that she was a passenger on the back of the bike. I asked Diana to find out if that was true. No, but the lady and her thirteen-year-old son had been in a similar accident earlier that morning. I then noticed the lady still had her IV stent in her arm.

We asked if she was in pain.
"Yes."
Could we pray for her?
"Yes." Diana had her repeat my healing prayer as we stood on the side of the road. *My healing belongs to me, because of what Jesus has done; I receive my healing, now.*

We asked her what she was feeling. No words came, just tears. All of the pain in her legs and arms was gone. This lady was with her son and another couple who had been in the restaurant. At seeing her friend instantly healed, the other lady asked if we could pray for her too. She had lower back and shoulder pain. She had the same reaction. She burst into tears before the prayer was even over. She began to repent to Jesus and call out to him. We just stood there amazed that God was healing people so quickly.

After we got back into our cars and resumed the journey into Medellin, we had a revelation. The reason why Natalie and Diana decided to go a longer route wasn't due to traffic, it was all about us being at the right place at the right time to minister to two ladies. We had been sensing, seeing, and hearing without great drama. We were in the flow of knowing God's will. Because Diana and I are both action people, we got to see two healings before we even got into the city.

WHAT IS A CHRISTIAN?

In Acts 11 we read the second of two stories that came about as a result of the persecution by Saul (Acts 8). The narrative tells us that at least two unnamed men headed to Antioch because their lives were threatened.

They must not have been listening to the sermons of their apostolic leaders because they broke several rules. Rule one was that Jews only evangelize Jews. Gentiles were dogs, so it was beneath us to even think about offering them the Good News. Well these men were either rule breakers or led by the Spirit, as they began to minister to Greeks. They started the first Gentile church, in Antioch. This church would go on to become the focal

point for world missions. It would be the platform from which Barnabas
and Paul would transform the Roman world.

Barnabas was rushed from Jerusalem to Antioch to oversee this new
church. He loved it and encouraged the people to keep doing what they
were doing. Barnabas recognized that this new Gentile church needed
some good Bible teaching. Seeing that he was more apostolic in nature,
Barnabas got the very man who had started the persecution to be their
teacher. He recruited Paul as his associate pastor (Acts 11:25–26). Something interesting is written at the summary of this story. We read that *they
were first called Christians in Antioch"* (Acts 11:26).

NICKNAMES

Nicknames stick. Especially when it comes to characterizing other cultures
and faith groups. Throughout history, we often have had negative names
for people from other countries. The same goes for differing denomina-
tions and faith groups.

For example, did you know that **Baptists** didn't name themselves? John
Calvin, who didn't like this group, gave Baptists their name.

A group of followers of Jesus in Switzerland were reading their Bibles.
They saw that baptism seemed to be more for those who had personally
chosen Jesus rather than a ritual for babies. So they baptized each other.
They were labeled Anabaptists (re-baptizers).

Time has shortened their name to Baptists (though modern, distinct Anabaptist theology does still exist). Why were they called Baptists? Because one of their unique customs was that they immersed people in water.

Did you know that **Pentecostals** didn't name themselves either? Well-meaning evangelicals who didn't understand speaking in tongues gave them the label. "You folks are just like the people on the day of Pentecost." The nickname stuck.

Methodists were also given a made-up name. John Wesley, the revivalist, wrote many discipleship books for his converts. He wrote methods on how to pray, methods on how to read the Bible, and methods on how to memorize Scripture. Other faith groups named that group Methodists.

The name *Christian* has a similar story. The word is made up of two Greek words meaning *little* and *Christ*. *Christ* means *anointed one*. Jesus was *the* anointed one. These people in Antioch were called little anointed ones. Why that name? Well, can I suggest that another rule was broken? The leaders of this church weren't any of the original Twelve. They felt to do church slightly different, perhaps because their church members were Gentiles rather than Jews.

What Barnabas and Paul did differently was to release all the congregants to do the "Jesus stuff." In the stories of the Jerusalem congregation, we read about the apostles' exploits for God; we don't see stories about them empowering everyone else to have a go. I believe that Barnabas and Paul had a revelation that God's heartbeat was that everyone should be able to live by faith, not just the "pastors." I believe that they taught their people

THE FAITH ZONE

how to tune to revelation and then do whatever Father God communicated. These believers in Antioch were characterized by the anointing. They were able to do the very same things that Jesus did with the anointing. The community of Antioch recognized this and tagged them with this new, made-up name: Christians.

THE PURPOSE OF THE ANOINTING

Friends, if Jesus lived by faith, and if the first mega church in Antioch taught their members to live this way, I think that this is the norm. You and I are to be seeing, hearing, and knowing what the Father wants. That is called hope. When we go the next step and act, well, now we are in the Faith Zone, where nothing is impossible.

Most of us treat church like an incubator. It is a safe place to practice praying for the sick. We get to develop our prophetic gift. We do dress rehearsals for when the meeting is over and we merge into our pagan secular neighbourhoods. But most of us live outside of the church context. We have jobs that take us into a very secular society. There isn't an incredible worship band playing in the background in our workplace. In fact, the environment that most of us work in is very humanistic. Crude jokes. Swearing is normal. The music that is playing in the background is contrary to all that we know to be right and honourable.

The anointing that each of us carries is and should be more visible in this environment. We should be standing out as lights in a dark place. The anointing on our lives is meant as a demonstration of God's love for the very people who don't yet know Jesus. I am by nature an introvert. I just have the wrong job title for one. As a pastor I need to be "on" most of the time. Getting outside myself has not been easy. I've had to learn to be outgoing. I've had ministry for the fear of man. I'm now at the place where I actively go to others. I can talk about Jesus; I can offer people free healing.

BIBLE SCHOOL JOB

When I was in Seminary I had a morning job before my classes. I worked for a food company that supplied food, beverages, newspapers, etc., for coffee trucks. These are the vehicles that drive into an industrial area or construction site, not the fancy food trucks that we see on downtown city streets. The trucks would start coming in about six in the morning and the last one left the warehouse about eight a.m. If the drivers slept in, or traffic was bad, tempers would flair. Three of us looked after getting the supplies to the trucks on time. One guy focused on coffee, one on the other beverages, and I was the food guy.

I had trays of sandwiches, muffins, donuts, cookies, etc., that trucks had ordered the day before. All of the food was made that night. The men wanted their supplies as fast as possible so they could get out and service their route. Pressure was placed on my team.

One man was always late. He was always miserable. He somehow felt that he should be treated better than the others. He wanted his supplies as soon as he drove in, even if we were in the middle of servicing another client. He yelled and cursed the three of us constantly. The two other guys, young adults like me, cursed back. I said nothing; I was a good Baptist. Day after day this happened.

One day this man drove in and as soon as he got out of his truck he yelled, "Steve, where the hell are you?" I was in the warehouse when someone pointed me out to him. I saw him coming. As he got closer he asked me said, "Steve, are you a Christian?" I responded that I was. This foul-mouthed bully then told me that his daughter was in the hospital. She'd been in a car accident the previous day.

"Could you say a prayer for her?"

Well, that changed our relationship right there. He never swore at me again. The other guys still got it every morning. Most mornings he was grateful that I helped him load his truck so he could head out and make money.

Here's my point: If doing nothing overtly as a follower of Jesus gets a reaction, what response would I get if I were to initiate the supernatural? What if I have a word of knowledge, or a prophetic word, and I get it right? What if my healing prayers work? I believe that these brand new Gentile believers in Antioch took their revelation to the streets. They acted on the ideas and thoughts they got; God-stuff happened.

This is how the church in Antioch got the reputation for being anointed. People put two and two together and thought, *They are almost as good as Jesus was; let's call them anointlings.* This is who we are. Little anointed ones, anointlings. At least, it is supposed to be who we are. Those who don't yet know Jesus are to understand that God is still alive and that Jesus is the way to the Father. How do they get this message? Through us.

Let me wrap this chapter up. Jesus, while being fully God, chose to be limited in the use of his divine powers. For the 33 years that he lived on earth, he had no unique links to God. He lived exactly like us.

HOW DID JESUS DO THE STUFF?

The secret to the miracles, healings, and the amazing insights that Jesus had has two parts.

First, his ability to receive revelation from the Father. He had dreams, thoughts, pictures, ideas, etc. Just like we do.

Second, his willingness to act on this revelation. Jesus always responded positively to what God revealed to him and he did it. He lived by faith.

As we look at the Gospel accounts of Jesus, we are to be inspired. We see how easy it can be to trust the revelatory ideas that come our way. If this is how Jesus lived, we can do the same. If Jesus saw amazing results from obeying his Father, we can see the same outcomes when we step out in faith!

Let's choose to act on revelation and enter the Faith Zone.

Father thank you that Jesus is our role model, our prototype. Every-
thing that he did supernaturally was because you first communicated
to him. He believed you and then went about doing what you said.
Father, help me to live this way. Thank you for the ideas, thoughts, and
insights that you reveal to me. Please give me more of them. Father,
help me to not fear what might or might not happen, but to choose to
act and do what you reveal to me. Help me to be a doer of your word
and not just a hearer. Amen.

GOING DEEPER

1. Jesus did what he saw. Ask the Lord to increase your ability to see in
   the spirit realm. Ask the Lord for more dreams and visions. Then *look*
   for visions all the time. They appear as gentle pictures that alight upon
   your mind. Honor these as visions from God.

2. Jesus did what he heard. Ask the Lord to increase your ability to hear
   in the spirit realm. Ask the Lord for more words of knowledge, random
   thoughts, audible voices, and quiet words. Recognize the voice of the
   Holy Spirit as flowing thoughts which alight upon your mind. Honor
   these as they come to you. Act on them.

3. Jesus did what he knew. Ask the Lord to increase your ability to know
   in the spirit realm. Ask the Lord for more insights, more wisdom, more
   understanding of what is really going on. Do what David did, picture
   the Lord constantly at your right hand (Acts 2:25; Psalm 16:8).

CHAPTER 13

Fears and Faith, First Cousins

MARK 5

When Jesus had again crossed over by boat to the other side of the lake, a large crowd gathered around him while he was by the lake. Then one of the synagogue leaders, named Jairus, came, and when he saw Jesus, he fell at his feet. He pleaded earnestly with him, "My little daughter is dying. Please come and put your hands on her so that she will be healed and live." So Jesus went with him. A large crowd followed and pressed around him.

While Jesus was still speaking, some people came from the house of Jairus, the synagogue leader. "Your daughter is dead," they said. "Why bother the teacher anymore?" Overhearing what they said, Jesus told him, "Don't be afraid; just believe." He did not let anyone follow him except Peter, James and John the brother of James. When they came to the home of the synagogue leader, Jesus saw a commotion, with people crying and wailing loudly. He went in and said to them, "Why all this commotion and wailing? The child is not dead but asleep." But they laughed at him. After he put them all out, he took the child's father and mother and the disciples who were with him, and went in where the child was. He took her by the hand and said to her, "Talitha koum." (which

means "Little girl, I say to you, get up."). Immediately the girl stood up and
began to walk around (she was twelve years old). At this they were completely
astonished. He gave strict orders not to let anyone know about this, and told
them to give her something to eat. MARK 5:21-43

As we conclude this book, I'd like to talk about what I think is the primary
challenge to living in the Faith Zone.

I don't believe the challenge is hearing from God. Every follower of Jesus
is wired to receive revelatory thoughts, pictures, dreams, and ideas from
our Father.

I don't believe daring to act is the issue. God gives us boldness, which is a
step up from courage. Courage is you and I acting like someone we aren't.
Boldness is when we step into our true identity and function in the anointing. The Holy Spirit gives us boldness when we ask (Acts 4:32).

The challenge is simple: we hear too easily from Satan.

In almost all of the stories that we have looked at from Matthew's gospel,
there has been a direct verbal challenge from Satan. Let's review.

Can God provide? Only one boy brought a bag lunch to the revival meeting where 43,000 showed up. Satan whispered to the disciples that it
would take a year's salary to buy everyone lunch. Satan's words caused
fear instead of a release of faith.

Can God protect? The disciples were not sure. Waves swept over the boat;
their lives were in danger. Satan's thoughts told them that they were going

to die right there in the middle of the Sea of Galilee. This caused fear in all of the disciples. No one was bold enough to squelch the storm; they had to wake Jesus and have him do something.

Can God heal? The bleeding lady from Capernaum hoped so. Satan probably reminded her that she had tried all the doctors. He reminded her that she was now poor and twelve years older. Satan reminded her that she wasn't allowed in public. Her challenge was to replace those thoughts with the God-thought: a touch would heal her.

Can God do miracles? Satan told the good people of Nazareth that miracles didn't happen any more. The lies they believed from Satan caused them to question the audacity of Jesus to come to their town to lead a miracle service. They responded with unbelief and doubt, rather than expectancy. They proved themselves right and no miracles happened that day.

DOUBT STARTED WITH ADAM AND EVE

The battle that most of us face every day is whether to listen to Satan or to listen to our Father. This is not new to us; it has been happening since God created Adam and Eve. God spoke clearly to Adam about the only restriction to living in the Garden of Eden.

> And the LORD God commanded the man, "You are free to eat from any tree in the garden; but you must not eat from the tree of the knowledge of good and evil, for when you eat from it you will certainly die" GENESIS 2:16–17

Apparently Satan was listening in. Shortly after, he talked to Adam and Eve and challenged everything that God said. (Some of you might have thought that Satan only talked to Eve—not so. Genesis 3:6 tells us that Adam was standing silently beside Eve the whole time. His sin, the first sin, was not covering and protecting his wife.)

> *"Did God really say, 'You must not eat from any tree in the garden'?" The woman said to the serpent, "We may eat fruit from the trees in the garden, but God did say, 'You must not eat fruit from the tree that is in the middle of the garden, and you must not touch it, or you will die.'" "You will not certainly die," the serpent said to the woman.* GENESIS 3:1-4

What just happened? Satan put doubt into the mind and heart of both Adam and Eve. Adam had clearly heard God's rules. He may or may not have communicated this to Eve. They both now hear Satan challenge God's words. Who will they listen to?

That is the pattern that Satan uses with us. He quickly undermines and twists the rhema words we get from Father God. He supplants them and tries to cancel them out. He does everything he can to cause us to pause, ponder, and doubt. This doubt cripples us from entering into the Faith Zone. Rather, it moves us into fear. Satan used this very same strategy to challenge Jesus during his forty-day fast. Three times Satan used the word *if* to undermine the identity and destiny of Jesus.

> *"If you are the Son of God, tell these stones to become bread."* MATTHEW 4:3

> *"If you are the Son of God,"* he said, *"throw yourself down."* MATTHEW 4:6

> *"If you will bow down and worship me."* MATTHEW 4:9

If Satan had the courage to speak to Jesus, then you and I are not exempt. All of us, like it or not, get an earful from Satan. For most of us it is a daily occurrence. If you are like me, it is almost hourly! Not good. The challenge we face is whom will we listen to. God's revelations can lead us into breakthroughs if we act. Satan's words lead us to doubt, fear, compromise, withdrawal, panic, depression, etc. The list is long.

FEAR COMES FROM ACTING ON SATAN'S REVELATIONS

Here is what I believe. Faith is acting on Father God's revelations. Fear comes when we act on Satan's revelations. In both cases we have a thought. One is from God and the other is from Satan. On the surface you'd think this would be a no brainer. Why would we give any attention to Satan if we know he's the one speaking? We'd choose God every time, wouldn't we?

Well, it sounds easy but it is a battle. Satan uses our weaknesses to gain his advantage. In the same way that a pack of lions knows which of the zebras is injured and targets that one, so Satan knows our weak spots. Our weak spot can be a previous traumatic experience. It can be sexual abuse. It can be physical hardships. It can be verbal abuse. It can be poverty and bankruptcy. It can be war and terrorism. It can be a broken heart, a broken relationship, or a broken marriage. It can be all of the above and a thousand more wounds.

One of the prime reasons the Apostle Paul teaches about inner healing in the Epistles is to help us get past our weak spots. Paul talks often about putting off all the negatives from our past and putting on the freedom that Jesus has to offer us.

Therefore, each of you must put off falsehood and speak truthfully to your neighbor, for we are all members of one body. "In your anger do not sin": Do not let the sun go down while you are still angry, and do not give the devil a foothold. EPHESIANS 4:25-27

THE STORY OF JAIRUS

Perhaps the most dramatic example of the battle of fear and faith is illustrated in the story of Jairus. The Bible narratives tell us that he was the ruler of the synagogue in Capernaum. This role would be the same as a chairman of a board of directors of a church or charity today.

We have no prior knowledge of this man. We can guess that he was a religious man because of his distinguished position. We don't know if he was a friend of Jesus or not. We do know that he had a big problem: a dying daughter.

Jairus, along with a large crowd, welcomes Jesus as he lands on the shore near Capernaum. We see his faith statement in Mark 5:23 as he approaches Jesus: *"My little daughter is dying. Please come and put your hands on her so that she will be healed and live."* Jairus humbles himself in front of the other town folks. He has had a revelation that all his daughter needs is a *touch*. Would Jesus come and *touch* his twelve-year-old daughter? The answer is yes.

A problem develops. You will recall in chapter six of this book that we talked about obstacles. A woman who has been haemorrhaging for twelve years delays Jesus from getting to Jairus' home. She touches Jesus as her act of faith and receives a tremendous healing. Good for her, but bad for Jairus, because this delays Jesus even more. It is even worse for Jairus' dying daughter—time is running out for her.

News comes that brings both Jairus and Jesus back to reality: the daughter's illness had been critical and she is now dead. The time spent ministering to the lady with the issue of blood may have killed any chance the twelve-year-old girl had of being healed.

> While Jesus was still speaking, some people came from the house of Jairus, the synagogue leader. "Your daughter is dead," they said. "Why bother the teacher anymore?" MARK 5:35

The day began with an act of faith. A revelation came to Jairus, or perhaps his wife. "If only Jesus was in town, he could help."

"A touch from Jesus will heal our beloved daughter."

Hope must have jumped sky high when they heard that Jesus was arriving at their town via boat.

Jarius acts on his revelation. He rushes to the shore, pushes past the other greeters, and finds Jesus. He asks him to touch his daughter. Jesus says yes. Hope is still high as they head to the home where the little girl is lying. Jairus and his wife believe for a miracle. Friends are also at the home praying. The intercessors know why Jairus has left the prayer vigil to get Jesus. Everyone is hopeful.

Remember the town has only 75 homes. Everyone knows Jesus. He owns one of the homes. They know that miracles and healings happen when Jesus is in town. There is great anticipation that Jesus will come to the home to touch the girl any moment now.

But not this time. The daughter is dead. Two men are sent from the home to have a quiet word with Jairus. They want to break the news to him privately before he arrives back to the house.

FEARS CHALLENGES FAITH

Notice the opportunities for fear to settle in for Jairus.

"Your daughter is dead." This is as big as it gets for most of us. Many of us have faith that God can provide. Some of us believe for our healings. But almost all of us give up hope when the person we are praying for dies.

"Why bother the teacher anymore?" The conclusion of Jairus' two neighbours is that there is no hope. It's over. She died and that is all there is to it. These friends haven't had the same personal revelation as Jairus did, so they resort to logic and reason. Dead means dead. It is hopeless.

So, whose faith is being challenged here?

I'm sure you quickly thought about Jairus and his wife. You are right, but there is one other person being challenged. That person is Jesus. Has Jesus raised someone from the dead? Not yet. Have resurrections being happening in Israel? Nope, not for the last 800 years. This may be a slight problem. To make matters more complicated for both Jairus and Jesus, they encounter a crowd of mourners when they turn the corner to the home.

The prayer vigil for her healing has turned into grieving cries,

> When they came to the home of the synagogue leader, Jesus saw a commotion, with people crying and wailing loudly. He went in and said to them, "Why all this commotion and wailing? The child is not dead but asleep." But they laughed at him. MARK 5:38-40

Two more obstacles for Jesus and Jairus.

People crying and wailing loudly. Nobody, not even close family, has any hope. They have all given up. The funeral preparations are in full swing. In Middle Eastern countries still to this today, most funerals take place within 24 hours.

They laughed at him. When Jesus utters a faith statement, *"Why all this commotion and wailing? The child is not dead but asleep,"* the people laugh. Laughing is not a good response when one is seeking to inspire hope. Mockery kills dreams very quickly.

JESUS ALWAYS REACTS TO OUR FAITH

The narrative tells us that Jesus now acts on the revelation that he has. I have already mentioned that Jesus responded to the faith of others.

We saw this in the story of the four men who brought their paralyzed friend to Jesus by opening the roof. I believe that when Jesus was approached by Jairus on the beach and heard his request, something kicked in for him. It is not in the text, but I believe that Father God said something like, "Go for it." So Jesus did. He began the walk to Jairus' home.

Jesus heard something from His Father. I know that for sure. Otherwise why did he walk to the home of a dead girl? Why did he utter that it was not over? Jesus stepped into the Faith Zone.

Remember, Philippians 2 tells us that Jesus, while fully God, totally functioned in his humanity. Jesus didn't have any advantages when it came to fears and faith. He heard Satan speaking doubt and he heard his Father speaking hope, just like us. Jesus agrees with Jairus' request and walks with him into Capernaum towards the home where the little girl is struggling to hold onto her life.

Jesus encourages Jairus not to give up when they get the news about her death.
Jesus doesn't retreat when he sees and hears the mourners.
Jesus pushes on when the laughing begins.
Jesus clears the house of all the doubters. *"After he put them all out, he took the child's father and mother and the disciples who were with him, and went in where the child was"* (Mark 5:40).
Jesus does what Jairus had originally asked him to do. He touches the girl. *"He took her by the hand and said to her, 'Talitha koum,'"* (which means "Little girl, I say to you, get up") (Mark 5:41).

A tremendous miracle happened that day. A twelve-year-old girl was raised from the dead by a touch and a two-word Hebrew prayer. This was the first time that Jesus had to believe for this type of miracle. Jesus went on from this experience to later raise a widow's son in Nain (Luke 7:11–17) and his friend Lazarus (John 11:38–44).

THE GREATEST BATTLE FOR FAITH THAT JESUS FACED

Do you remember the several hours that Jesus spends in Gethsemane praying? The Scriptures tell us that it was agonizing (Matthew 26:36–46). Hematidrosis, the medical term for bloody sweat, only happens under intense stress. It happened to Jesus. What was this stressful battle about?

Jesus was trying to hear from his Father about an alternate finish to the cross (Matthew 26:39, 42). Was there another option? Did Jesus have to die? Did he have to suffer the agony of the scourging from the Roman officers? Did he have to be nailed to a cross? Did he have to take on our sins and be cursed for dying on a tree?

I believe that part of the stress as Jesus prayed among the olive trees was this: Would he be forever separated from his Father? Would he be raised from the dead? Who would be the one to believe for the impossible for him? He couldn't count on any of his Twelve; one of them had already turned to Satan. Twice he asked those who were still with him to pray, and twice they had fallen asleep. Who would be there for him?

Imagine with me. Jesus is praying and as he looks over his shoulder he sees his buddies; they are sleeping. The doubts surely came. If I can't count on them to pray with me for an hour, can I trust them when the circumstances really heat up? I think Jesus is feeling that he can't depend on them. So who would care for him and raise him from the dead? Would one of the women, perhaps one of the Marys, have the confidence to push in for his resurrection?

I believe that one of the reasons Father God allowed Jesus to raise people from death was to convince him that his own resurrection was also possible. He had to make the choice and face the cross. Jesus had to make the choice to live by faith. Paul tells us in 1 Corinthians 10:13 that Jesus was tempted with the very same temptations that we all face. He wasn't exempt from any. Temptation is Satan putting one of his thoughts in your mind. Tempting thoughts are very similar to doubting thoughts.

You and I never know when a tempting thought is about to come. We don't choose the time, Satan does. It's the same with doubt. Satan plants thoughts at key moments in our lives.

Elijah had doubts when Jezebel cursed him. Right after one of his most spiritually "on" days, he was filled with suicidal thoughts. He had just called down fire from heaven and the prophets of Baal killed (1 Kings 18:38). Satan chooses the times to press the doubt button, not us. Now, a day later, fresh from the highs of a spiritual victory, Elijah got a word from Jezebel, the king's wife (1 Kings 19:2).

"You're a dead man"

What happened next? Instead of holding onto the words of the Lord, he valued what this pagan woman's words as more important and more truthful. Doubt invaded his mind, fears entered, and he ran for his life. Why? He listened to the wrong voice.

Our battle is the same. Good things happen and Satan gives his spin. Bad things happen and Satan gives his take. Each time, we are forced to make a decision: Do I listen to Father God (hope) or to my enemy (doubt)? Do I act on hope and enter the Faith Zone, or do I act on doubt and enter the fear zone? We get to choose.

A WARNING

There is an interesting warning that Jesus gave to the good people of Capernaum on one of his visits. *"And you, Capernaum, will you be lifted to the heavens? No, you will go down to Hades. For if the miracles that were performed in you had been performed in Sodom, it would have remained to this day"* (Matthew 11:23). Why the warning?

Capernaum had seen more miracles than any other town where Jesus ministered. Jesus knew that Satan would challenge the people and introduce doubt. Satan would be seeking to undermine what had happened the previous three years. Jesus was warning them to continue to live in faith rather than doubt. That same warning is for us today.

What will we do when an obstacle comes our way that challenges what our Father has spoken to us about?

What will we do when a thought comes into our mind that confronts the very revelation God gave us?

This is our daily challenge.

I have been convicted recently by the Holy Spirit as to whether I am a follower of Jesus or not. Let me explain.

If I'm a child of Father God and a follower of Jesus, why do I follow Satan more? Why do I listen to him more than I do my Heavenly Father? Sadly, I'm ashamed to say that much of my day consists of giving in to the doubts Satan plants. I step back. I hesitate. I don't act on what my Father has spoken, on what I know. I forget that if God said it, it is possible. By my actions, it appears that I am a more frequent follower of Satan than I am of Jesus. This is not good! I've been crying out to God to help me in this. I want to only follow Jesus.

Friends, this is one of our biggest struggles. Will we step into the super-natural realm where anything is possible to those who believe? Or will we revert to logic, man's wisdom, and succumb to doubt?

As we conclude this book, I'd love for you to do a couple journal exercises. But first let me pray for you.

Father, my friend wants to be an active child of God and follower of Jesus. I'm guessing that they too struggle often with aligning themselves with Your words over Satan's. Father, please forgive us for all of the times when we know we have heard from you and done nothing. Forgive us for the times when we have chosen to listen to Satan. Forgive us for receiving doubt and living in fear. Father, we want to live in the Spirit. We want to be led by your wonderful Holy Spirit. We want to hear you and be doers of your rhema words. We want to live in the Faith Zone. Father come now; cleanse us and refresh us. Breathe life into our spirits again. May we choose you each day. May we listen and then do what you speak to us to do. May we act on your revelation. May we show you and everyone else that we are your children who hear your voice. May we represent you and bring your kingdom to this world. Amen.

GOING DEEPER

1. Ask the Lord to remind you of the last time you gave into doubt. Why did you do that? What was the key reason you listened to Satan rather than Father God? Record what He says.

2. Ask the Lord to remind you of a time when you had doubt but still acted on what God said. What was the reason you listened to Father rather than Satan? Record what He says.

3. Ask the Lord what He'd like to say to you today in response to reading this chapter. Record and do what He says.

Do not merely listen to the (revelatory) word, and so deceive yourselves. Do what it says. JAMES 1:22

APPENDIX 1:   HOW TO HEAR GOD'S VOICE,
BY MARK & PATTI VIRKLER

She had done it again! Instead of coming straight home from school like she was supposed to, she had gone to her friend's house. Without permission. Without our knowledge. Without doing her chores.

With a ministering household that included remnants of three struggling families plus our own toddler and newborn, my wife simply couldn't handle all the work on her own. Everyone had to pull their own weight. Everyone had age-appropriate tasks they were expected to complete. At fourteen, Rachel and her younger brother were living with us while her parents tried to overcome lifestyle patterns that had resulted in the children running away to escape the dysfunction. I felt sorry for Rachel, but, honestly my wife was my greatest concern.

Now Rachel had ditched her chores to spend time with her friends. It wasn't the first time, but if I had anything to say about it, it would be the last. I intended to lay down the law when she got home and make it very clear that if she was going to live under my roof, she would obey my rules.

But... she wasn't home yet. And I had recently been learning to hear God's voice more clearly. Maybe I should try to see if I could hear anything from Him about the situation. Maybe He could give me a way to get her to do what she was supposed to (what I wanted her to do). So I went to my office and reviewed what the Lord had been teaching me from Habakkuk 2:1, 2 NASB: *"I will stand on my guard post and station myself on the rampart; And I will keep watch to see what He will speak to me...Then the Lord answered me and said, 'Record the vision....'"*

Habakkuk said, "*I will stand on my guard post...*" (Habakkuk 2:1). The first key
to hearing God's voice is to go to a quiet place and still our own thoughts
and emotions. Psalm 46:10 encourages us to be still, let go, cease striving,
and know that He is God. In Psalm 37:7 we are called to "*be still before the
Lord and wait patiently for Him.*" There is a deep inner knowing in our spirits
that each of us can experience when we quiet our flesh and our minds.
Practicing the art of biblical meditation helps silence the outer noise and
distractions clamoring for our attention.

I didn't have a guard post but I did have an office, so I went there to quiet
my temper and my mind. Loving God through a quiet worship song is one
very effective way to become still. In 2 Kings 3, Elisha needed a word from
the Lord so he said, "Bring me a minstrel," and as the minstrel played, the
Lord spoke. I have found that playing a worship song on my autoharp is
the quickest way for me to come to stillness. I need to choose my song
carefully; boisterous songs of praise do not bring me to stillness, but rather
gentle songs that express my love and worship. And it isn't enough just
to sing the song into the cosmos—I come into the Lord's presence most
quickly and easily when I use my godly imagination to see the truth that
He is right here with me and I sing my songs to Him, personally.

"I will keep watch to see," said the prophet. To receive the pure word of
God, it is very important that my heart be properly focused as I become
still, because my focus is the source of the intuitive flow. If I fix my eyes
upon Jesus (Hebrews 12:2), the intuitive flow comes from Jesus. But if I fix
my gaze upon some desire of my heart, the intuitive flow comes out of that
desire. To have a pure flow I must become still and carefully fix my eyes

upon Jesus. Quietly worshiping the King and receiving out of the stillness that follows quite easily accomplishes this.

So I used the second key to hearing God's voice: As you pray, fix the eyes of your heart upon Jesus, seeing in the Spirit the dreams and visions of Almighty God. Habakkuk was actually looking for vision as he prayed. He opened the eyes of his heart, and looked into the spirit world to see what God wanted to show him.

God has always spoken through dreams and visions, and He specifically said that they would come to those upon whom the Holy Spirit is poured out (Acts 2:1–4, 17).

Being a logical, rational person, observable facts that could be verified by my physical senses were the foundations of my life, including my spiritual life. I had never thought of opening the eyes of my heart and looking for vision. However, I have come to believe that this is exactly what God wants me to do. He gave me eyes in my heart to see in the spirit the vision and movement of Almighty God. There is an active spirit world all around us, full of angels, demons, the Holy Spirit, the omnipresent Father, and His omnipresent Son, Jesus. The only reasons for me not to see this reality are unbelief or lack of knowledge.

In his sermon in Acts 2:25, Peter refers to King David's statement: "*I saw the Lord always in my presence; for He is at my right hand, so that I will not be shaken.*" (NASB) The original psalm makes it clear that this was a decision of David's, not a constant supernatural visitation: "*I have set* (literally, I have placed) *the Lord continually before me; because He is at my right hand,*

I will not be shaken" (Psalm 16:8 NASB). Because David knew that the Lord was always with him, he determined in his spirit to see that truth with the eyes of his heart as he went through life, knowing that this would keep his faith strong.

In order to see, we must look. Daniel saw a vision in his mind and said, *"I was looking...I kept looking...I kept looking"* (Daniel 7:2, 9, 13 NASB). As I pray, I look for Jesus, and I watch as He speaks to me, doing and saying the things that are on His heart. Many Christians will find that if they will only look, they will see. Jesus is Emmanuel, God with us (Matthew 1:23). It is as simple as that. You can see Christ present with you because Christ *is* present with you. In fact, the vision may come so easily that you will be tempted to reject it, thinking that it is just you. But if you persist in recording these visions, your doubt will soon be overcome by faith as you recognize that the content of them could only be birthed in Almighty God.

Jesus demonstrated the ability of living out of constant contact with God, declaring that He did nothing on his own initiative, but only what he saw the Father doing, and heard the Father saying (Jn. 5:19,20,30). What an incredible way to live!

Is it possible for us to live out of divine initiative as Jesus did? Yes! We must simply fix our eyes upon Jesus. The veil has been torn, giving access into the immediate presence of God, and he calls us to draw near (Luke 23:45; Hebrews 10:19-22). *"I pray that the eyes of your heart may be enlightened...."* (Ephesians 1:18 NASB)

When I had quieted my heart enough that I was able to picture Jesus without the distractions of my own ideas and plans, I was able to "keep watch to see what He will speak to me." I wrote down my question: "Lord, what should I do about Rachel?"

Immediately the thought came to me, "She is insecure." Well, that certainly wasn't my thought! Her behavior looked like rebellion to me, not insecurity.

But like Habakkuk, I was coming to know the sound of God speaking to me (Habakkuk 2:2). Elijah described it as a still, small voice (1 Kings 19:12). I had previously listened for an inner audible voice. While God does speak that way at times, I have found that usually God's voice comes as spontaneous thoughts, visions, feelings, or impressions. For example, have you ever been driving down the road and had a thought come to you to pray for a certain person? Didn't you believe it was God telling you to pray? What did God's voice sound like? Was it an audible voice, or was it a spontaneous thought that lit upon your mind?

Experience indicates that we perceive spirit-level communication as spontaneous thoughts, impressions and visions, and Scripture confirms this in many ways. For example, one definition of *paga*, a Hebrew word for intercession, is "a chance encounter or an accidental intersecting." When God lays people on our hearts, he does it through *paga*, a chance-encounter thought "accidentally" intersecting our minds.

So the third key to hearing God's voice is recognizing that God's voice in your heart often sounds like a flow of spontaneous thoughts. Therefore, when I want to hear from God, I tune to chance-encounter or spontaneous thoughts.

Finally, God told Habakkuk to record the vision (Habakkuk 2:2). This was not an isolated command. The Scriptures record many examples of individual's prayers and God's replies, such as the Psalms, many of the prophets, and Revelation. I have found that obeying this final principle amplified my confidence in my ability to hear God's voice so that I could finally make living out of His initiatives a way of life. The fourth key, two-way journaling or the writing out of your prayers and God's answers, brings great freedom in hearing God's voice.

I have found two-way journaling to be a fabulous catalyst for clearly discerning God's inner, spontaneous flow, because as I journal I am able to write in faith for long periods of time, simply believing it is God. I know that what I believe I have received from God must be tested. However, testing involves doubt and doubt blocks divine communication, so I do not want to test while I am trying to receive (see James 1:5–8). With journaling, I can receive in faith, knowing that when the flow has ended I can test and examine it carefully.

So I wrote down what I believed He had said: "She is insecure." But the Lord wasn't done. I continued to write the spontaneous thoughts that came to me: "Love her unconditionally. She is flesh of your flesh and bone of your bone."

My mind immediately objected: She is not flesh of my flesh. She is not related to me at all—she is a foster child, just living in my home temporarily. It was definitely time to test this "word from the Lord"!

There are three possible sources of thoughts in our minds: ourselves, Satan and the Holy Spirit. It was obvious that the words in my journal did not come from my own mind—I certainly didn't see her as insecure or flesh of my flesh. And I sincerely doubted that Satan would encourage me to love anyone unconditionally!

Okay, it was starting to look like I might have actually received counsel from the Lord. It was consistent with the names and character of God as revealed in the Scripture, and totally contrary to the names and character of the enemy. So that meant that I was hearing from the Lord, and he wanted me to see the situation in a different light. Rachel was my daughter—part of my family not by blood but by the hand of God Himself. The chaos of her birth home had created deep insecurity about her worthiness to be loved by anyone, including me and including God. Only the unconditional love of the Lord expressed through an imperfect human would reach her heart.

But there was still one more test I needed to perform before I would have absolute confidence that this was truly God's word to me: I needed confirmation from someone else whose spiritual discernment I trusted. So I went to my wife and shared what I had received. I knew if I could get her validation, especially since she was the one most wronged in the situation, then I could say, at least to myself, "Thus sayeth the Lord."

Needless to say, Patti immediately and without question confirmed that the Lord had spoken to me. My entire planned lecture was forgotten. I returned to my office anxious to hear more. As the Lord planted a new, supernatural love for Rachel within me, he showed me what to say and how to say it to not only address the current issue of household responsibility, but the deeper issues of love and acceptance and worthiness.

Rachel and her brother remained as part of our family for another two years, giving us many opportunities to demonstrate and teach about the Father's love, planting spiritual seeds in thirsty soil. We weren't perfect and we didn't solve all of her issues, but because I had learned to listen to the Lord, we were able to avoid creating more brokenness and separation.

The four simple keys that the Lord showed me from Habakkuk have been used by people of all ages, from four to a hundred and four, from every continent, culture and denomination, to break through into intimate two-way conversations with their loving Father and dearest Friend. Omitting any one of the keys will prevent you from receiving all he wants to say to you. The order of the keys is not important, just that you use them all. Embracing all four, by faith, can change your life. Simply quiet yourself down, tune to spontaneity, look for vision, and journal. He is waiting to meet you there.

You will be amazed when you journal! Doubt may hinder you at first, but throw it off, reminding yourself that it is a biblical concept, and that God is present, speaking to his children. Relax. When we cease our labors and enter his rest, God is free to flow (Hebrews 4:10).

Why not try it for yourself, right now? Sit back comfortably, take out your pen and paper, and smile. Turn your attention toward the Lord in praise and worship, seeking His face. Many people have found the music and visionary prayer called "A Stroll Along the Sea of Galilee" helpful in getting them started. You can listen to it and download it free at CWGMinistries. org/galilee.

After you write your question to him, become still, fixing your gaze on Jesus. You will suddenly have a very good thought. Don't doubt it; simply write it down. Later, as you read your journaling, you, too, will be blessed to discover that you are indeed dialoguing with God. If you wonder if it is really the Lord speaking to you, share it with your spouse or a friend. Their input will encourage your faith and strengthen your commitment to spend time getting to know the Lover of your soul more intimately than you ever dreamed possible.

Five ways to be sure what you're hearing is from God:

1. **Test the Origin (1 John 4:1)**

   Thoughts from our own minds are progressive, with one thought leading to the next, however tangentially. Thoughts from the spirit world are spontaneous. The Hebrew word for true prophecy is *naba*, which literally means to bubble up, whereas false prophecy is *ziyd* meaning to boil up. True words from the Lord will bubble up from our innermost being; we don't need to cook them up ourselves.

2. **Compare It to Biblical Principles**

   God will never say something to you personally which is contrary to his universal revelation as expressed in the Scriptures. If the Bible clearly states that something is a sin, no amount of journaling can make it right. Much of what you journal about will not be

specifically addressed in the Bible, however, so an understanding
of biblical principles is also needed.

3. Compare It to the Names and Character of God as Revealed in the Bible

Anything God says to you will be in harmony with his essential
nature. Journaling will help you get to know God personally, but
knowing what the Bible says about him will help you discern what
words are from him. Make sure the tenor of your journaling lines up
with the character of God as described in the names of the Father,
Son and Holy Spirit.

4. Test the Fruit (Matthew 7:15-20)

What effect does what you are hearing have on your soul and your
spirit? Words from the Lord will quicken your faith and increase
your love, peace and joy. They will stimulate a sense of humility
within you as you become more aware of who God is and who you
are. On the other hand, any words you receive which cause you to
fear or doubt, which bring you into confusion or anxiety, or which
stroke your ego (especially if you hear something that is "just for
you alone—no one else is worthy") must be immediately rebuked
and rejected as lies of the enemy.

5. Share It with Your Spiritual Counselors (Proverbs 11:14)

We are members of a Body! A cord of three strands is not easily
broken and God's intention has always been for us to grow together.
Nothing will increase your faith in your ability to hear from God like
having it confirmed by two or three other people! Share it with your

spouse, your parents, your friends, your elder, your group leader, even your grown children can be your sounding board. They don't need to be perfect or super-spiritual; they just need to love you, be committed to being available to you, have a solid biblical orientation, and most importantly, they must also willingly and easily receive counsel. Avoid the authoritarian who insists that because of their standing in the church or with God, they no longer need to listen to others. Find two or three people and let them confirm that you are hearing from God!

APPENDIX 2:   PHOTOS OF CAPERNAUM

An aerial view of Capernaum, in the Galilee, and the Lake of Galilee.
Photo taken by Mordagan for the Israeli Ministry of Tourism

Mordagan. *Capernaum: Aerial View.* Digital image. *Israeli Ministry of Tourism.* Flickr, 9 June 2000. Web. 6
    Apr. 2016. <https://www.flickr.com/photos/israelphotogallery/14529764071/in/photostream/>.

Ruins of the old Roman town.
Photo taken by David Shankbone

Shankbone, David. *Ruins of the Old Roman Town.* Digital image. *Capernaum.* Wikipedia, 30 Nov. 2007.
    Web. 6 Apr. 2016. <https://en.wikipedia.org/wiki/Capernaum>.

APPENDIX 3:   THE FAITH PROCESS CHART

MINISTRY STORIES RELATING TO FAITH			
Scripture	Person/Group	Problem	Revelation
Matthew 4:23-25	Crowd	Ill with diseases	"news about him"
Matthew 8:1-4	One Leper	leprosy	"If you are willing you can make me clean"
Matthew 8:5-13	Centurion	paralyzed servant	"I myself am a man under authority"
Matthew 8:14-15	Peter's Mother-in-Law	fever	
Matthew 8:16-17	Crowd	demon possessed	people were brought to Jesus (based on the ministry in the synagogue)
Matthew 8:23-27	The Twelve	Sea of Galilee storm	we need Jesus to do something
Matthew 9:1-8	Four Friends	paralyzed friend	get him to Jesus, through the roof
Matthew 9:18-19, 23-26	Jairus	daughter has died	"Put your hand on her and she will live"
Matthew 9:20-22	Lady	bleeding for 12 years	touch the hem of his clothes
Matthew 9:27-31	Two Blind Men	blind	Jesus can restore their sight
Matthew 9:32-34	Mute Man	demon possessed and mute	he was brought to Jesus by the town's people
Matthew 12:9-14	Synagogue	shriveled hand	"How much more valuable is a person than a sheep?"
Matthew 12:22-23	Crowd	blind and mute man	people brought him to Jesus
Matthew 13:54-58	Nazareth	doubt, dishonour	we know who he is

Obstacle	Action	Miracle	Characterization
traveled from Syria	people brought to Jesus all who were ill	Jesus healed them all	
unclean, needs to keep distance from people	came and knelt before Jesus	cleansed of his leprosy	
	just say the word	servant healed instantly from a distance	great faith
	Jesus touched her	fever left her, she got up and waited on them	
no one was set free in the Old Testament	drove out the spirits with a word	healed all the sick	
"We are going to drown"	rebuked the wind and waves	immediately calm seas	little faith
can't get close to Jesus because of the crowd	dug up the roof and lowered him	forgiven and healed instantly	saw their faith
child is dead (dying according to the other passages)	took the girl by the hand	and she got up	
crowd, social and religious restrictions	touched the hem	instantly healed	your faith healed you
missed the meeting, closed door	went into the house to find Jesus	instantly healed	according to your faith be it done unto you
		mute spoke	
Sabbath day	told the man to stretch his arm out	it was completely restored	
no blind were healed in the Old Testament	Jesus healed him	he could talk and see	
the carpenter's son	took offense at Jesus	no miracles	no faith

MINISTRY STORIES RELATING TO FAITH (continued)

Scripture	Person/Group	Problem	Revelation
Matthew 14:13-21	The Twelve	no food	Jesus says "Let us feed them"
Matthew 14:25-33	The Twelve	Sea of Galilee storm	Jesus says "Come"
Matthew 14:34-36	Crowd	sickness	it we touch Jesus we will be healed
Matthew 15:21-28	Cannanite Woman	daughter is demonized	just a crumb is all that is needed, Gentiles don't have to wait for miracles
Matthew 15:29-39	The Twelve	no food	Jesus says "I have compassion for these people"
Matthew 17:14-20	The Twelve	boy with seizures	Jesus says "All you needed was faith the size of a mustard seed"
Matthew 20:29-34	Large Crowd	two blind men	"We want our sight"

TEACHING ON FAITH

Scripture	Person/Group	Problem	Revelation
Matthew 6:25-34	Crowd		We are more valuable to God than birds are, He looks after then, He will look after us
Matthew 16:5-12	The Twelve	no food	we forgot to bring bread
Matthew 21:18-22	The Twelve	no figs on a tree	no figs means the tree is deceitful

Obstacle	Action	Miracle	Characterization
year's salary	have the people sit in 50s	5000+ were fed plus leftovers	
wind and waves	got out of the boat	walked on water	little faith
	sent word to everyone, touched Jesus	all were healed	
silence, timing, insults	called out, pushed in, argued with Jesus	daughter was instantly healed	great faith
no where to purchase food	gave thanks, broke them, gave them to the Twelve	4000+ were fed plus leftovers	
resistant spirits	didn't push in	none	little faith
	Jesus had compassion and touched their eyes	Immediately they received their sight	

Obstacle	Action	Miracle	Characterization
Worry - what will we eat?	Seek His kingdom and His righteousness	everything is added to us	little faith
	grumbled	none	little faith
	Jesus cursed the tree	immediately the tree withered	if you have faith and do not doubt

A God who
loves you

wants you to
experience him

be transformed

and given
power

At Catch The Fire, we are passionate about seeing people be transformed by a living God. We have many books that can help you on your journey, but we are also involved in much more.

Why not join us at a conference or seminar this year? Or come on a short-term mission with us? Or have your heart radically changed at a 5-month school. Or just visit one of our churches in many cities around the world.

CONTINUE YOUR JOURNEY AT
catchthefirebooks.com/whatsnext

ALSO AVAILABLE FROM

CATCH THE FIRE BOOKS

MY HEALING BELONGS TO ME

STEVE LONG

My Healing Belongs to Me is a simple, practical guide to receiving healing and ministering healing to others! Packed with clear Biblical truth, it contains a lifetime of exciting stories of God healing everything from leprosy to death itself. Steve Long presents all that the Bible has to say about healing, to provide the most effective tools for ministering to the sick.

ALSO AVAILABLE FROM

CATCH THE FIRE BOOKS

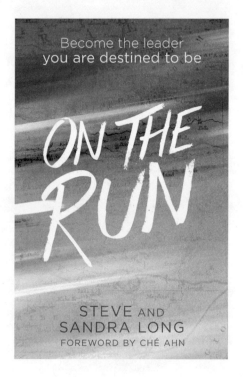

Become the leader
you are destined to be

ON THE RUN

STEVE AND
SANDRA LONG
FOREWORD BY CHÉ AHN

ON THE RUN

STEVE AND SANDRA LONG

Join the ride as Steve & Sandra Long take us through David's thrilling wilderness journey to undergo a crash course in leadership preparation that each of us will benefit from. Full of memorable storytelling and keen insight, *On The Run* is a leadership guide for the rest of us.

ALSO AVAILABLE FROM
CATCH THE FIRE BOOKS

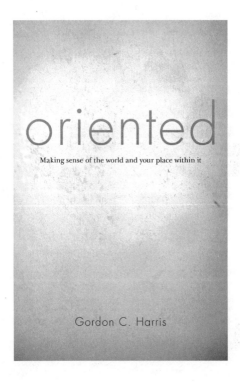

oriented

Making sense of the world and your place within it

Gordon C. Harris

ORIENTED

GORDON C. HARRIS

Oriented is a compelling journey through the events, characters and stories of early Genesis that frames our understanding of God, the world, and our lives.

Go Arsenal